From the Bible-Teaching Ministry of

CHARLES R. SWINDOLL

You and Your Money

LifeMaps

Insight for Living

YOU AND YOUR MONEY
A LifeMaps Book

From the Bible-Teaching Ministry of Charles R. Swindoll

Charles R. Swindoll has devoted his life to the clear, practical teaching and application of God's Word and His grace. A pastor at heart, Chuck has served as senior pastor to congregations in Texas, Massachusetts, and California. He currently pastors Stonebriar Community Church in Frisco, Texas, but Chuck's listening audience extends far beyond a local church body. As a leading program in Christian broadcasting, *Insight for Living* airs in major Christian radio markets around the world, reaching people groups in languages they can understand. Chuck's extensive writing ministry has also served the body of Christ worldwide and his leadership as president and now chancellor of Dallas Theological Seminary has helped prepare and equip a new generation for ministry. Chuck and Cynthia, his partner in life and ministry, have four grown children and ten grandchildren.

Published By:
IFL Publishing House
A Division of Insight for Living
Post Office Box 251007
Plano, Texas 75025-1007

You and Your Money was collaboratively developed by Creative Ministries of Insight for Living.
Writer for chapters two and four: Derrick G. Jeter, Th.M., Dallas Theological Seminary
Editor in Chief: Cynthia Swindoll, President, Insight for Living
Executive Vice President: Wayne Stiles, Th.M., D.Min., Dallas Theological Seminary
Theological Editor: John Adair, Th.M., Ph.D., Dallas Theological Seminary
Content Editor: Amy L. Snedaker, B.A., English, Rhodes College
Copy Editors: Jim Craft, M.A., English, Mississippi College
      Kathryn Merritt, M.A., English, Hardin-Simmons University
Project Coordinator, Creative Ministries: Melanie Munnell, M.A., Humanities,
      The University of Texas at Dallas
Project Coordinator, Communications: Sarah Magnoni, A.A.S., University of Wisconsin
Proofreader: Paula McCoy, B.A., English, Texas A&M University-Commerce
Designer: Kari Pratt, B.A., Commercial Art, Southwestern Oklahoma State University
Production Artist: Nancy Gustine, B.F.A., Advertising Art, University of North Texas

ISBN: 978-1-57972-918-9
Printed in the United States of America

Table of Contents

A Letter from Chuck

As a preacher, I know how hazardous it is to bring up the subject of money. People get nervous. Their arms get crossed. They hear the words *money, tithing,* and *stewardship* coming from the lips of a Bible-thumper, and they run for the doors . . . one hand on their wallets. I can relate to that reaction. I understand why folks worry when preachers turn to the topic of money. We have the "health and wealth" guys to thank for that. These charlatans have poisoned the well of trust between the pew and the pulpit. Their heretical teaching claims that God's blessings are for sale—for the right price . . . or the best bargain. They masquerade as God's commissioned salesmen to dispense over-the-top blessings. They're salesmen all right—selling snake oil and hogwash!

Truth be told, God's blessings aren't for sale. He gives them to whomever He chooses. They're gifts of grace. But just because God's blessings can't be bought with money doesn't mean that money matters aren't important to God—they are. In fact, the making and managing of money was important to God long before it became important to us. You see, God owns everything. He told Moses on Mount Sinai "the whole earth is mine" (Exodus 19:5 NIV). Not part of the earth; not half of the earth; not three-quarters or seven-tenths of the earth — the *whole* earth belongs to God! One hundred percent. Out of this vast treasury of riches, the Lord gives gifts and calls upon us to manage those gifts His way, to accomplish His purposes, always for His glory. This is stewardship.

The book you hold in your hands will not offer you some pie-in-the-sky nonsense or suggest that God and His blessings can be bought. Rather, it will challenge you to think biblically about this important topic. We've titled this volume *You and Your Money*, but remember: it really isn't yours. Once you've been set free from the love of money, you'll be free to give generously and with great joy as the Lord directs you.

So, don't slam this book shut and run for the door! (You don't even have to worry about your wallet.) Find a comfortable place to sit with your Bible, and allow God to encourage you with the truth that both you and your money belong to Him.

Charles R. Swindoll

Charles R. Swindoll

At its heart, a map is the distillation of the experience of travelers—those who have journeyed in the past and recorded their memories in the form of pictures and symbols. The map represents the cumulative wisdom of generations of travelers, put together for the benefit of those now wishing to make that same journey.

To undertake a journey with a map is therefore to rely on the wisdom of the past. It is to benefit from the hard-won knowledge of those who have explored the unknown and braved danger in order to serve those who will follow in their footsteps. Behind the lines and symbols of the map lie countless personal stories—stories the map itself can never tell. Yet sometimes those stories need to be told, just as the hard-won insights of coping with traveling can encourage, inspire, and assist us.[1]

—Alister E. McGrath

Welcome to LifeMaps

On a journey, the important thing is not speed as much as it is *direction*.

But sometimes heading the right way requires some guidance. Think about it. You would never set out on a long road trip without first making sure you knew which direction to go, right? You'd consult a map. For many people, the journey toward a deeper and more meaningful relationship with God lies along new or unfamiliar ground. They need directions; they need a map. And, even with a map, sometimes you can still get lost. When you do, it's the locals who know best—those who have been down the same roads. That's why this book is designed to be completed in concert with someone else. Wise friends or counselors can encourage us in our spiritual growth and help us avoid pitfalls along our paths.

Using LifeMaps

LifeMaps provides opportunities for individuals to interact with the Bible in different settings and on several levels, depending upon your particular needs or interests. *LifeMaps* also places a tool in the hands of pastors and other Christian leaders, helping them guide others along a journey of spiritual growth through the study and application of the Bible.

For Individuals

You can use *LifeMaps* in your personal devotionals to gain God's perspective on a particular area of Christian living. In addition to offering engaging chapters to read, *LifeMaps* can further your journey of spiritual growth with the help of penetrating questions and opportunities for personal application.

LifeMaps can also serve as a first step to healing or resolving an issue that continues to plague you. Read, reflect, answer the questions, and then contact a competent, mature, godly man or woman to discuss the topic as it relates to your personal situation. This individual can be a pastor, a counselor, a friend, or even one of our staff here at Insight for Living in Pastoral Ministries. (See page 91 for information on how to contact Insight for Living.) This step is an essential part of the journey.

For Pastors and Counselors

LifeMaps is designed to guide individuals through an engaging, in-depth study of the Word of God, freeing you to help them apply the truths in even more specific and personal ways. As a vital first step in the counseling process, each volume lays a solid, biblical, theological, and practical foundation upon which you can build. Encouraging individuals to work through the book on their own allows them the time necessary for personal reflection and education while enabling you to target your ministry of personal interaction and discipleship to their particular needs.

For Groups

LifeMaps can serve as a curriculum for home Bible studies, Sunday school classes, and accountability or discipleship groups. Each book in the series contains enough material for group discussion of key questions and noteworthy passages. *LifeMaps* can also foster meaningful interaction for pastors, elders, staff, and Christian leaders.

Suggestions for Study

Whether you use *LifeMaps* in a group, in a counseling setting, in the classroom, or for personal study, we trust it will prove to be an invaluable guide as you seek deeper intimacy with God and growth in godliness. In any setting, the following suggestions will make *LifeMaps* more beneficial for you.

- Begin each chapter with prayer, asking God to teach you through His Word and to open your heart to the self-discovery afforded by the questions and text.

- Read the chapters with pen in hand. Underline any thoughts, quotes, or verses that stand out to you. Use the pages provided at the end of each section to record any questions you may have, especially if you plan to meet with others for discussion.

- Have your Bible handy. In chapters 2 and 4, you'll be prompted to read relevant sections of Scripture and answer questions related to the topic.

- As you complete each chapter, close with prayer, asking God to apply the wisdom and principles to your life by His Holy Spirit. Then watch God work! He may bring people and things into your life that will challenge your attitudes and actions. You may gain new insight about the world and your faith. You may find yourself applying this new wisdom in ways you never expected.

May God's Word illumine your path as you begin your journey. We trust that this volume in the *LifeMaps* series will be a trustworthy guide to learning and to your spiritual growth.

You and Your Money

Chapter 1

Strengthening Your Grip on Money

Now *there's* a fitting title! Especially in a day when our checking accounts need month-to-month resuscitation to survive mind-numbing government deficits and debts. Unlike those who receive incredible salaries for playing games, making movies, singing songs, and pumping oil, most of us are forced to face the fact that the only way we'll ever see daylight is to moonlight. Even then we feel like nothing more than members of the *debt* set. So when somebody mentions that there is a way to strengthen our grip on money, we listen.

Don't misunderstand. I'm in no way interested in promoting greed. We get enough of that mercenary jungle-fighting on the job every day. And the flame of materialism is fanned anew each evening, thanks to the commercials that relentlessly pound their way into our heads. But even though we may get weary of that drumbeat, none can deny that money plays an enormous role in all our lives . . . even when we keep our perspective and steer clear of greed. As is often said, money cannot bring happiness—but it certainly puts our creditors in a better frame of mind.

I agree with the late heavyweight champ, Joe Louis: "I don't like money, actually, but it quiets my nerves." [1]

The Bible Talks about Money

To the surprise of many people, the Bible says a great deal about money. It talks about earning and spending, saving and giving, investing and even wasting our money. But in none of this does it ever come near to suggesting that money brings ultimate security. I love the proverb that paints this so vividly:

> Do not wear yourself out to get rich;
>> have the wisdom to show restraint.
>
> Cast but a glance at riches, and they
>> are gone, for they will surely sprout
>> wings and fly off to the sky like an
>> eagle. (Proverbs 23:4–5 NIV)

Can't you just picture the scene? WHOOSH . . . and the whole thing is gone for good.

This is not to say that money is evil. Or that those who have it are wicked. Let's once for all put to bed the old cliché: "God loves the poor and hates the rich." Nowhere does God condemn the rich for being rich. For sure, He hates false gain, wrong motives for getting rich, and lack of compassionate generosity among the wealthy. But some of the godliest people in the Bible were exceedingly prosperous, even by today's standards: Job, Abraham, Joseph, David, Solomon, Josiah, Barnabas, Philemon, and Lydia, to name a few.

In my observation, both the prosperous and those without abundance must fight similar battles: envy of others and greed for more. Scripture clearly and frequently condemns both attitudes. This brings to mind a particular section of the Bible that addresses several of the attitudes that frequently accompany money.

Ancient Counsel That Is Still Reliable

In 1 Timothy, a letter written to a young man who was a pastor, the writer (Paul) dealt with the subject of money as he drew his thoughts to a close. While encouraging Timothy to carry on in spite of the odds against him, Paul exposed some of the characteristics of a religious fraud in chapter 6, verses 4 and 5:

> He is conceited and understands
> nothing; but he has a morbid interest
> in controversial questions and disputes
> about words, out of which arise envy,
> strife, abusive language, evil suspicions,
> and constant friction between men of
> depraved mind and deprived of the
> truth, who suppose that godliness is a
> means of gain. (1 Timothy 6:4–5)

The Message renders the latter part of verse 5: "They think religion is a way to make a fast buck."

Red flag! Keen-thinking Paul used this as a launching pad into one of the most helpful discussions of money in all the Bible. Read carefully these words that follow:

> But godliness actually is a means
> of great gain when accompanied by
> contentment. For we have brought
> nothing into the world, so we cannot
> take anything out of it either. If we have
> food and covering, with these we shall
> be content.

But those who want to get rich fall into temptation and a snare and many foolish and harmful desires which plunge men into ruin and destruction. For the love of money is a root of all sorts of evil, and some by longing for it have wandered away from the faith and pierced themselves with many griefs. . . .

Instruct those who are rich in this present world not to be conceited or to fix their hope on the uncertainty of riches, but on God, who richly supplies us with all things to enjoy. Instruct them to do good, to be rich in good works, to be generous and ready to share, storing up for themselves the treasure of a good foundation for the future, so that they may take hold of that which is life indeed. (1 Timothy 6:6–10, 17–19)

Go back and check that out. The first series of thoughts is a *reminder* to those without much money. The second section is a *warning*. The third is simply *instruction*. Let's dig deeper.

Reminder to Those Who Are Not Rich (1 Timothy 6:6–8)

Picking up the term "godliness" from verse 5, Paul mentioned it again in the next verse, linking it with contentment and offering a primary formula . . . a basic premise for happiness:

Godliness + Contentment = Great Gain

Meaning:

A consistent, authentic walk with God

+ An attitude of satisfaction and peace within (regardless of finances)

—————————————————————

That which constitutes great wealth

If there were one great message I could deliver to those who struggle with not having an abundance of this world's goods, it would be this simple yet profound premise for happiness. For a moment, let's go at it backward, from bottom to top.

That which constitutes great wealth is not related to money. It is an attitude of satisfaction ("enough is enough") coupled with inner peace (an absence of churning) plus a day-by-day, moment-by-moment walk with God. Sounds so simple, so right, so good, doesn't it? In our world of more, more, more . . . push, push, push . . . grab, grab, grab, this counsel is long overdue. In a word, the secret is *contentment*.

Consider Philippians 4:11–12:

> Not that I speak from want, for I have learned to be content in whatever circumstances I am. I know how to get along with humble means, and I also know how to live in prosperity; in any and every circumstance I have learned the secret of being filled and going hungry, both of having abundance and suffering need.

Contentment is something we must learn. It isn't a trait we're born with. But the question is *how?* Back in the 1 Timothy 6 passage, we find a couple of very practical answers to that question:

1. A current perspective on eternity: "For we have brought nothing into the world, so we cannot take anything out of it either" (1 Timothy 6:7).

2. A simple acceptance of essentials: "If we have food and covering, with these we shall be content" (6:8).

Both attitudes work beautifully.

First, reading the eternal dimension into today's situation can really help us quit striving for more. We entered life empty-handed; we leave it the same way. I never saw a hearse pulling a U-Haul trailer!

The truth of all this was brought home forcefully to me when a minister friend of mine told of an experience he had several years ago. He was in need of a dark suit to wear at a funeral he had been asked to conduct. He had very little money, so he went to a local pawn shop in search of a good buy. To his surprise, they had one just the right size, solid black, and very inexpensive. It was too good to be true. As he forked over the money, he inquired as to how they could afford to sell the suit so cheap. With a wry grin, the pawnbroker admitted that all their suits had once been owned by a local mortuary, which meant they had been used on the deceased . . . then removed before burial.

The minister felt a little unusual wearing a suit that had once been on a dead man, but since no one else would know, why not? Everything was fine until he was in the middle of his sermon and casually started to stick his hand into the pocket of the pants . . . only to find *there were no pockets*! Talk about an unforgettable object lesson! There he stood preaching to all those people about the importance of living in light of eternity today, as he himself wore a pair of trousers without pockets that had been on a corpse.

Second, boiling life down to its essentials and trying to simplify our lifestyles helps us model contentment. Verse 8 spells out those essentials: something to eat, something to wear, and a roof over our heads. Everything beyond that we'd do well to consider as extra.

You see, society's plan of attack is to create dissatisfaction, to convince us that we must be in a constant pursuit for something "out there" that is sure to bring us happiness. When you reduce that lie to its lowest level, it is saying that contentment is impossible without striving for more. God's Word offers the exact opposite advice: contentment is possible when we *stop* striving for more. Contentment never comes from externals. Never!

As a Greek sage once put it: "To whom little is not enough, nothing is enough." [2]

In the *Third Part of King Henry the Sixth*, Shakespeare drew a picture of the king wandering alone in the country, where he meets two men who recognize him as the king. One of them asks, "But, if thou be a king, where is thy crown?" The king gives a splendid answer:

> My crown is in my heart, not on my
> > head;
> Not deck't with diamonds and Indian
> > stones,
> Nor to be seen; my crown is call'd
> > content;
> A crown it is that seldom kings enjoy. [3]

Great story, but I'll be frank with you. My bottom-line interest is not the words of some Greek sage or the eloquent answer of a king borne in the mind of an English poet. It's *you*. It's helping you see the true values in life, the exceedingly significant importance of being contented with what you have rather than perpetually dissatisfied, always striving for more and more. I am certainly not alone in this desire to help people see through the mask of our world system:

> PROMISES, PROMISES. Perhaps the most devastating and most demonic part of advertising is that it attempts to persuade us that material possessions will bring joy and fulfillment. "That happiness is to be attained through limitless material acquisition is denied by every religion and philosophy known to man, but is preached incessantly by every American television set." Advertisers promise that their products will satisfy our deepest needs and inner longings for love, acceptance, security and sexual fulfillment. The right deodorant, they promise, will bring acceptance and friendship. The newest toothpaste or shampoo will make one irresistible. A house or bank account will guarantee security and love.
>
> Examples are everywhere. A bank in Washington, D.C., advertised for new savings accounts with the question: "Who's gonna love you when you're old and grey?"

For a decade, my own savings bank used a particularly enticing ad: "Put a little love away. Everybody needs a penny for a rainy day. Put a little love away." Responsible saving is good stewardship. But promising that a bank account guarantees love is unbiblical, heretical, and demonic. This ad teaches the big lie of our secular, materialistic society. But the words and music are so seductive that they dance through my head hundreds of times.

If no one paid any attention to these lies, they would be harmless. But advertising has a powerful effect on all of us, and it shapes the values of our children.

In a sense we pay too little attention to advertisements. Most of us think we can ignore them, but in fact they seep into the subconscious. We experience them instead of analyze them. John V. Taylor suggested that Christian families ought to adopt the slogan "Who are you kidding?" and shout it in unison every time a commercial appears on the telelvision screens. [4]

It really works. My whole family and I tried it one afternoon during a televised football game. Not once did I feel dissatisfied with my present lot or sense the urge to jump up and go buy something. Our dog almost had a canine coronary; but, other than that, the results were great.

Warning to Those Who Want to Get Rich (1 Timothy 6:9–10)

As we read on, Scripture turns our attention from those who are not rich to those who want to get rich. The warning is bold:

> But those who want to get rich fall
> into temptation and a snare and many
> foolish and harmful desires which
> plunge men into ruin and destruction.
> For the love of money is a root of all
> sorts of evil, and some by longing for it
> have wandered away from the faith and
> pierced themselves with many griefs.
> (1 Timothy 6:9–10)

This person is different from the first one we considered. This individual is one who cannot rest, cannot really relax until he or she has become affluent. The word *want* in verse 9, rather than meaning "like" or "desire" (like a passing fancy), suggests a firm resolve, a strong determination. It isn't an exaggeration to suggest that *want* would even include the idea of being possessed with the thought of getting rich. This definition helps us understand why such a severe warning follows: those who *want* to get rich fall into temptation (unexpected traps) and many foolish or harmful desires leading ultimately to destruction.

Interestingly, contrary to popular opinion, the pursuit of wealth—even the acquiring of it—does not cause the bluebird of happiness to sing its way into our lives. Rather, the grim, diseased vulture of torment and misery circles over our carcasses.

You need a 'fer instance?

Look at the faces of the super wealthy. Choose the group. Entertainers, *offstage*. How about rock stars? Or even comedians away from the camera? Let's name a few specifics: Lindsay Lohan, O. J. Simpson, Michael Jackson. Those faces, captured in untold numbers of photographs, reflect strain and pain. And let's not forget the stress-ridden physician or executive pushing toward the top. Not much peace and calm, in my opinion.

Let's look at what Solomon said:

> A faithful man will be richly blessed,
> > but one eager to get rich will not go
> > unpunished. . . .
> A stingy man is eager to get rich
> > and is unaware that poverty awaits
> > him. (Proverbs 28:20, 22 NIV)

Why? Why is the path of the greedy materialist so strewn with blind spots and traps that lead to ruin? Read again 1 Timothy 6:10, but don't *misread* it.

> For the love of money is a root of all
> sorts of evil, and some by longing for it
> have wandered away from the faith and
> pierced themselves with many griefs.
> (1 Timothy 6:10)

The verse does not say that money per se is a root of all evil, nor that the love of money is *the* root of all evil. This has reference to the LOVE of money (literally, "fondness of silver") being *a* (not "the") root—a basis of all kinds of evil. The verse also describes the kind of person who pursues money as one who is "longing for it." The original Greek means, "To stretch oneself out in order to grasp something." And those on this pursuit experience two categories of perils:

- Spiritually, they wander away from the faith.

- Personally, they encounter many griefs.

It's worth remembering that most people with this kind of drive for more and more money really aren't generous; they are selfish. One writer put it all in perspective:

> Money in itself is neither good nor bad; it is simply dangerous in that the love of it may become bad. With money a man can do much good; and with money he can do much evil. With money a man can selfishly serve his own desires; and with money he can generously answer to the cry of his neighbor's need. With money a man can buy his way to the forbidden things and facilitate the path of wrongdoing; and with money he can make it easier for someone else to live as God meant him to live. Money brings power, and power is always a double-edged thing, for it is powerful to good and powerful to evil.[5]

The Bible offers two kinds of counsel: preventive and corrective . . . assistance before the fact and assistance after the fact. This verse is the former—a preventive warning. It stands like a yellow highway sign in a driving rainstorm.

DANGER, CURVE AHEAD

DRIVE SLOWLY

- Up-and-coming young executive, listen!

- Entertainer in the making, pay attention!

- Capable, youthful athlete, watch out!

- Recording artist, be careful!

- Visionary leader and entrepreneur, proceed with caution!

- Rapidly advancing salesperson, be on guard!

- Gifted minister with a lot of charisma, stop and think!

If you are not careful, you'll find yourself caught in the vortex of greed that will inevitably lead to your destruction. Materialism is a killer; at best, a crippler. Fight against it as you would a hungry pack of wolves.

Instruction to Those Who Are Rich (1 Timothy 6:17–19)

Consider one more classification deserving of our attention—those who have been blessed with prosperity. If you are in this category, you have your own unique battles. As I mentioned earlier in the chapter, you are neither suspect nor guilty in God's eyes simply because you are rich. You know if you acquired your wealth legally or illegally. If it has come from hard work, honest dealings, and wise planning, you have absolutely nothing of which to be ashamed. Only the Lord Himself knows how many ministries could not continue (humanly speaking) if not for people like you who are able to contribute large sums of money in support of these faith ventures. You are greatly blessed, and that carries with it great responsibility. As the object of innumerable attacks from the Adversary (not to mention the envy of many people), you must be a wise servant of what God has entrusted into your care. I know of few paths filled with more dangerous traps and subtle temptations than the one you must walk every day. Hopefully, these things will help you as you attempt to live for Christ on that precarious tightrope.

To begin, let's hear what Scripture says to you:

> Instruct those who are rich in this present world not to be conceited or to fix their hope on the uncertainty of riches, but on God, who richly supplies us with all things to enjoy. Instruct them to do good, to be rich in good works, to be generous and ready to share, storing up for themselves the treasure of a good foundation for the future, so that they may take hold of that which is life indeed. (1 Timothy 6:17–19)

If you look closely, you'll find three rather direct pieces of advice, the first two being negative and the third ending on a positive note.

First, Don't Be Conceited

This is a tough assignment, but it's essential. The term *conceited* means "high-minded." Proud, snobbish arrogance has no place in the life of the wealthy Christian. Because this is mentioned first, it is perhaps wise that we look upon it as the most frequent temptation the rich must guard against. One of the best ways to do that is to remember that everything you have has come from your heavenly Father. If it weren't for Him, think of where you'd be today. It's healthy for all of us to remember the hole of the pit from which He rescued us. That will do a lot to keep conceit conquered.

Marian Anderson, the African-American contralto who deserved and won worldwide acclaim as a concert soloist, didn't simply grow great; she grew great simply. In spite of her fame, she remained the same gracious, approachable woman . . . never one to "put on airs"—a beautiful model of humility.

A reporter, while interviewing Miss Anderson, asked her to name the greatest moment in her life. The choice seemed difficult to others who were in the room that day, because she had had many big moments. For example:

- There was the night Conductor Arturo Toscanini announced, "A voice like hers comes once in a century."

- In 1955, she became the first black American to sing with the Metropolitan Opera Company of New York.

- The following year her autobiography, *My Lord, What a Morning*, was published . . . a bestseller.

- In 1958, she became a United States delegate to the United Nations.

- On several occasions during her illustrious career, she received medals from various countries around the world.

- There was that memorable time she gave a private concert at the White House for the Roosevelts and the King and Queen of England.

- Her hometown, Philadelphia, had, on one occasion, awarded her the $10,000 Bok Award as the person who had done the most for that city.

- In 1963, she was awarded the coveted Presidential Medal of Freedom.

- There was that Easter Sunday in Washington D.C. when she stood beneath the Lincoln statue and sang for a crowd of 75,000, which included Cabinet members, Supreme Court justices, and most members of Congress.

Which of those big moments did she choose? None of them. Miss Anderson quietly told the reporter that the greatest moment of her life was the day she went home and told her mother she wouldn't have to take in washing anymore.[6]

The princely prophet Isaiah reminded us to do this very thing when he said:

> "Look to the rock from which you
> were hewn
> And to the quarry from which you
> were dug." (Isaiah 51:1)

That sounds much more noble and respectable than its literal meaning. In the Hebrew text, the word *quarry* actually refers to "a hole." The old King James Version doesn't miss it far: "the hole of the pit whence ye are digged." Never forget "the hole of the pit."

What excellent advice! Before we get all enamored with our high-and-mighty importance, it's a good idea to take a backward glance at the "hole of the pit" from which Christ lifted us. And let's not just *think* about it; let's admit it. Our "hole of the pit" has a way of keeping us all on the same level — recipients of grace. And don't kid yourself; even those who are extolled and admired have "holes" from which they were dug.

With Moses, it was murder.

With Elijah, it was deep depression.

With Peter, it was public denial.

With Samson, it was recurring lust.

With Thomas, it was cynical doubting.

With Jacob, it was deception.

With Rahab, it was prostitution.

With Jephthah, it was his illegitimate
    birth.

Marian Anderson never forgot that her roots reached
back into poverty. No amount of public acclaim ever
caused her to forget that her mama took in washing
to put food in little Marian's tummy. I have the feeling
that every time she started to get exaggerated ideas of
her own importance, a quick backward glance at her
humble beginnings was all it took to conquer conceit.
And the best part of all was that she didn't hide her
humble roots.

The next time we're tempted to become puffed
up by our own importance, let's just look back to the
hole of the pit from which we were dug. It has a way of
deflating our pride.

Second, Don't Trust in Your Wealth for Security

Earlier in the chapter, we looked at the proverb that
talks about riches sprouting wings and flying away. How
true! Foolish indeed is the person who considers himself
or herself safe and sound because he or she has money.
Part of the reason it is foolish is because the value of our
money is decreasing at a frightening rate of speed. As
the verse states, money is "uncertain."

And another reason it's foolish to trust in riches for security is that money, in the final analysis, brings no lasting satisfaction, certainly not in the area of things that really matter. There are many things that no amount of money can buy. Think of it this way:

> Money can buy medicine but not health.
>
> Money can buy a house but not a home.
>
> Money can buy companionship but not friends.
>
> Money can buy entertainment but not happiness.
>
> Money can buy food but not an appetite.
>
> Money can buy a bed but not sleep.
>
> Money can buy a crucifix but not a Savior.
>
> Money can buy the good life but not eternal life.

That explains why we are told in this section of Scripture that it is God (alone) who is able to supply us "with all things to enjoy." As Seneca, the Roman statesman once said: "Money has never yet made anyone rich."

Third, Become a Generous Person

Look at 1 Timothy 6:18–19 one more time:

> Command them to do good, to be rich in good deeds, and to be generous and willing to share. In this way they will lay up treasure for themselves as a firm foundation for the coming age, so that they may take hold of the life that is truly life. (NIV)

It is so clear it hardly needs an explanation. Woven through the fabric of these words is the same term: *give, give, give, give, give*.

You have money? Release it; don't hoard it. Be a great-hearted person of wealth. Let generosity become your trademark. Be generous with your time, your efforts, your energy, your encouragement, and, yes, your money.

Do you know what will happen? Along with being enriched, knowing that you are investing in eternity, you will "take hold of the life that is truly life." You will go beyond "the good life" and enter into "the *true* life." There is a vast difference between the two.

Review and Reminder

We haven't exhausted the subject of money, but we have addressed several critical issues. To those who struggle to make ends meet, guard against being envious of the wealthy and work on being content with life as it is.

To those who would have to admit that the pursuit of money is now a passionate drive, hear the warning again: if you don't come to terms with yourself, it's only a matter of time before you'll find yourself ensnared and miserable. In the process, you'll lose the very things you think money will buy—peace, happiness, love, and satisfaction.

And to those who are rich? Put away conceit, forget about finding ultimate security in your money, and cultivate generosity . . . tap into "the true life."

During His life on earth, Jesus frequently talked about those things that kept people from a meaningful relationship with God. One of the barriers, according to Jesus's teaching, is money. It need not be, but it often is.

- Jesus taught that "the deceitfulness of riches" has a way of choking the truth of Scripture, making it unfruitful in a life (Mark 4:19).

- He also taught that we need to be on "guard against every form of greed," since life really doesn't consist of the things we possess (Luke 12:15).

- He even went so far as to say, "For where your treasure is, there your heart will be also" (Luke 12:34).

- But the punch line in all His teaching on this subject says it all: "You cannot serve both God and Money" (Matthew 6:24 NIV).

Straight talk, but that's what it takes to strengthen our grip on money. Tell me, are you gripping it or is it gripping you?

My Questions and Thoughts

My Questions and Thoughts

_____

_____

_____

_____

_____

_____

_____

_____

_____

_____

_____

_____

_____

_____

_____

_____

_____

_____

_____

_____

_____

_____

_____

_____

Chapter 2

God Owns It All

You Are Here

Oscar Wilde, the Irish playwright and novelist, had a keen sense of human folly and wrote with understated humor. In *The Picture of Dorian Gray*, Wilde placed in the mouths of two characters this exchange of wisdom, "Young people, nowadays, imagine that money is everything. . . . And when they grow older they know it."[1]

Perhaps no one has better expressed her attitude about money than the late jazz and vaudeville singer Sophie Tucker: "From birth to eighteen a girl needs good parents; from eighteen to thirty-five she needs good looks; from thirty-five to fifty-five she needs a good personality, and from fifty-five on she needs cash."[2]

When it comes to money, it's hard to overestimate its allure or its importance. But money isn't everything— really, it isn't. However, we only come to that conclusion by changing the way we look at money. We must believe that God owns it all.

Discovering the Way

The Beatles represented many ideas we're better off not adopting, but when they sang "Can't Buy Me Love," they got the essence of money right. Money can buy many wonderful things in life, but it can't buy the most wonderful thing. However, if we're

23

completely honest, when it comes to money and material possessions, too many of us would have to admit that we love our stuff too much. And love like that means we're owned by the stuff we own. Like slaves serving an unrelenting master, we spend our lifetimes making money so we can buy stuff that grows ratty or breaks down and needs repair. And then we have to make more money to replace or repair all the old stuff. And so it goes — the vicious cycle seems never-ending. Oh, if only we could find a way of escape!

What is your honest opinion of or attitude toward your money?

_____

_____

_____

_____

Have you ever felt like a slave to your "stuff"? If so, why do you think that is?

_____

_____

_____

_____

How have you attempted to escape the slavery of money? How successful have those attempts been?

_____

_____

_____

_____

_____

Four Simple Words That Bring Financial Freedom

Most people, when they hear someone of financial means say, "Money isn't that important," think, *Yeah, right. That's easy for you to say!*

The fact is, money *is* important—and serious business. Sociologist Os Guinness wrote, "In an obvious sense we take money too seriously today. But less obviously, we do so only because we don't take money seriously enough—seriously enough to understand it."[3]

It's a lack of understanding that leads many into financial bondage. If you feel shackles tightening around your wallet, you need the freedom that comes from understanding the truth behind four simple words. The words aren't all that profound, but their truth is. Here they are: *God owns it all.*

"God owns it all" could be written across each of the following Bible passages, but read each one and write down specifically what God does own.

Exodus 19:5

_____

_____

_____

_____

Deuteronomy 10:14

_____

_____

_____

_____

Psalm 24:1

_____

_____

_____

_____

Psalm 50:10–11

_____

_____

_____

_____

1 Corinthians 6:19

_____

_____

_____

_____

What does God own? Everything! Paul wrote:

> For we have brought nothing into the
> world, so we cannot take anything out
> of it either. (1 Timothy 6:7)

All that we have is God's. We came into this world with empty hands, and we'll leave this world with empty hands. We take nothing with us. God owns it all.

John Wesley put it this way, "When the Possessor of heaven and earth brought you into being, and placed you in this world, he placed you here not as a proprietor, but a steward."[4]

Stewardship is managing God's treasures in God's way, for God's purposes, and always for God's glory. We begin life with our hands wide open, nothing in them. As we mature, God, by His grace, allows certain things to be placed into our possession, but not one of them is under our ownership. Remember, He owns everything in heaven and earth. It's all His.

So, in pleasing Him, we live our lives with open hands. We accept what He entrusts to us only as stewards, never as owners. We dare not think of gripping the things He entrusts to us. We hold everything loosely. We simply maintain the treasures He entrusts to us, investing them wisely but never forgetting that it is His sovereign right to remove those things from us any time He wants. That time may be in the middle of our lives when we feel the most prosperous. It may be early in our lives when we think we have earned the right to make a lot and to spend a lot. It may be later in life when the nest egg is broken and we have little to look forward to except an empty nest.

We're back to where we started: *God owns it all*. You will never be in financial distress if you remember those four words. They will revolutionize your thinking on finances. How great it would be if "God owns it all" could appear on every checkbook, every pocketbook, every income tax return, every stock transaction, every credit card, every home mortgage, every car title, every real estate contract, and every business deal. What a helpful reminder it would be if all the stuff in our homes—including our houses—were stamped with those four simple words.

A Gracious Reminder to a People Who Forgot

In their abundance, the Corinthians forgot that God owned it all. Shortly before Paul wrote his second letter to them, the Corinthians had been moved by the plight of the church in Jerusalem (Romans 15:26). Yet the fundraising campaign for the Jerusalem church had ground to a halt. A year before, the Corinthians had been excited about the cause of meeting the needs in Jerusalem. They had championed it. They had applauded it. But then their passion cooled and they abandoned it.

The Corinthians' failure to finish the task of collecting money prompted Paul to write:

> Here's what I think: The best thing you can do right now is to finish what you started last year and not let those good intentions grow stale. Your heart's been in the right place all along. You've got what it takes to finish it up, so go to it. (2 Corinthians 8:10–11 MSG)

 Read 2 Corinthians 8:7–9.

In an effort to motivate the Corinthians to finish what they started, Paul offered three incentives.

First, Paul encouraged them to *stop and consider the blessings of God* (2 Corinthians 8:7). If the Corinthians had opened their ledger of blessings, they would have discovered that they were "in the black" when it came to faith, solid biblical teaching, knowledge, zeal for the things of God, and love—and also apparently great financial blessing.

Read Psalm 103:1–5. What did David command his soul to do in verses 1–2? Is the command limited only to his soul? Explain.

_____

_____

_____

_____

What had God done for David, according to verses 3–5?

_____

_____

_____

_____

What is the benefit of obeying this command, according to verse 5?

_____

_____

_____

_____

When we remember that God owns it all and are grateful that He allows us to steward His blessings, then generosity becomes a gift because God continues to satisfy our needs and frees us from financial fears.

Here's the second incentive: _listen to the testimony of others_ (2 Corinthians 8:8). You could circle or underline the word "others" in verse 8 and draw a line to "the churches of Macedonia" in verse 1. The Macedonians were destitute by comparison, yet their giving to the Jerusalem church "overflowed in the wealth of their liberality" (8:2).

Generosity often produces more blessings in the lives of the givers than in the lives of those who receive. Many have testified: generosity brings blessings mere dollars and cents never could. This is true because the generous understand that their money isn't really theirs. They also understand that giving out of "the sincerity of . . . love" (2 Corinthians 8:8) returns an "abundance of joy" from God (8:2).

The third incentive: *look at the example of Christ* (8:9). In Colossians 1:16, Paul affirmed that Christ created "all things . . . both in the heavens and on earth." Jesus owned it all—all the diamond mines and oil fields and gold deposits of the world. How rich Jesus was . . . before He took on human flesh. When He gave it all up for the Corinthians—and for us—to become a pauper, He bought for us a treasure no amount of money could ever buy—eternal life.

Have you received the great treasure of eternal life as an inheritance? If not, or if you're not sure but would like to find out about this treasure, please read "How to Begin a Relationship with God" on page 85.

Read Philippians 2:5–8, and answer the following questions.

How did Paul describe Christ before the incarnation in verse 6?

_____

_____

_____

_____

How did Paul describe Christ's incarnation in verse 7?

_____

_____

_____

_____

What Christlike quality did Paul identify in verse 8, and how did he describe that quality?

_____

_____

_____

_____

What did Paul command in verse 5?

_____

_____

_____

_____

So, how are you doing in the humility department? Explain.

_____

_____

_____

_____

Money has never made anyone rich. The humble know this and confess that God owns it all, making it easy to give away money when God leads. They've come to see the reality that their poverty is really prosperity, so they follow the example of the One who owned it all but humbled Himself and set it aside. What an example to follow!

Read 2 Corinthians 8:10–15.

The Corinthians were Sunday-morning givers and Monday-morning hoarders. They had begun a good work but let it peter out before completion. Paul was a realist. He knew human nature was difficult to overcome, especially when it came to giving money. Therefore, Paul addressed four hindrances to generosity in his reminder to the Corinthians.

The first hindrance to generosity is *procrastination.* Webster defines the word as putting "off intentionally and habitually . . . something that should be done."[5] The Corinthians were initially passionate about helping the church in Jerusalem, but they had let a year dribble away in inactivity (2 Corinthians 8:10). *Tomorrow is another day; we'll get around to it then* was their attitude. "No," Paul said, in effect, "get around to it today; now finish doing what you began a year ago. Complete the task" (8:11). The answer to procrastination is *today — now!*

Hesitation is the second hindrance to generosity. This is the procrastinator's excuse for inaction: "I'm just not ready." The Corinthians had been ready a year before, but their enthusiasm for the project waned (8:11). However, Paul said, "If the readiness [would again become] present" — if they could get excited about blessing others financially — then God would bless whatever they could afford to give. The Corinthians didn't need to feel ashamed if they couldn't give as much as others — look at the poor Macedonians — for no one can give out of what they don't have, only out of what they do have (8:12). Paul offered the Corinthians a message of liberation, not comparison.

This feeling of inadequacy is at the heart of the third hindrance: *overreaction*. All of us have some ability to give, but the person who overreacts says, "I can't afford much, and the little I could give wouldn't make a dent in a tin pot. So why give at all?" Some will always have more money, and some will always give more. That's not the issue. Paul's point in 2 Corinthians 8:11–12 has nothing to do with the amount of the gift but with the attitude of the giver. Remember, God owns it all . . . whether your bank account is large or small.

Read Mark 12:41–44, and answer the following questions.

Who are the "players" in this scene? Who is the audience?

The players: _____

The audience: _____

What were the rich people putting into the treasury? And what did the widow put in?

The rich: _____

The widow: _____

In what way did the widow "put in more" than the rich? Explain.

_____

_____

_____

What lesson can we learn from this scene in the treasury?

_____

_____

_____

The fourth hindrance to generosity is the attitude of *exception* — that somehow we're exempt from God's plan of giving. Paul said to the Corinthians that giving to the needs of the Jerusalem church wasn't meant to drain them dry but to establish an "equality" (2 Corinthians 8:13). Paul didn't have in mind a financial equality — he wasn't trying to "spread the wealth" — but an equal *willingness* to carry the burden of others. The Corinthians' current "abundance" could help "supply . . .[the Jerusalem church's] need." And there may come a day, Paul reminded them, when the "abundance" of the church at Jerusalem would "supply . . . [the Corinthian church's] need" (8:14). If and when that day came, there would be "equality" — a willingness to help in kind. And in both cases, whatever amount, whether great or small, would be provided by God for the relief of the other, just as it was when the people gathered manna in the wilderness (8:15). God would ensure there was enough.

How generous do you consider yourself?

Tightfisted   Openhanded

1	2	3	4	5

If you're closer to the "tightfisted" end of the scale, what hindrances are keeping you from opening your hands? (Check all that apply.)

Procrastination	
Hesitation	
Overreaction	
Exception	

Read 2 Corinthians 8:16–24.

Turning our attention away from the giver and toward the receiver of gifts, we glean two principles related to who should handle money and how.

The first principle: *only qualified people should handle financial matters.* Paul sent three men — Titus and two unnamed brothers — to collect the money the Corinthians were sure to give for the Jerusalem church. Titus and the others were trustworthy because of their "earnestness" for the Corinthians to finish the collection (2 Corinthians 8:16). In fact, Titus paid his own expenses to travel to Corinth to collect the gift for the Jerusalem church (8:17). But more than that, these three men were appointed by the churches for the task and were under the churches' authority (8:19–20). As to these men's character, Paul said they had been tested and had been "found diligent in many things" (8:22). Finally, all three had labored for the sake of the gospel and the glory of Christ (8:18, 23).

The giving of money is no trivial business; neither should be the receiving of money. We should only entrust our gifts into the hands of faithful, capable, and qualified individuals. Remember, God owns it all, so those who receive our gifts should be trustworthy stewards of His resources.

The second principle: *money matters should be administered honestly and openly.* When people give their money to churches, ministries, and charities, they trust that their money will be used wisely and carefully. That trust is just as valuable as the money — maybe even more —

so it must be guarded. Paul assured the Corinthians that their gift for the Jerusalem church was in safe hands and would be used just as promised. After all, Paul told them, "We have regard for what is honorable, not only in the sight of the Lord, but also in the sight of men" (2 Corinthians 8:21). Paul wanted the Corinthians not to fear that their monies would be squandered or stolen; he urged them to finish what they started, for their gift would prove their love for the suffering Christians in Jerusalem—as well as prove that Paul had good reason to boast in the Corinthian church (8:24).

Starting Your Journey

For many people, money has become a god. If we're not careful—whether we're rich or poor—money can dominate our lives. One of the greatest challenges and the greatest blessings of life is to live with an open hand—to live generously. How generous are you? If you're struggling with greed or fear—the incessant grabbing or gripping of money and possessions—you will find great freedom when you come to terms with the fact that God owns it all.

Do you *really* believe that God owns it all? Do your actions reveal your belief? Elaborate.

_____

_____

_____

_____

_____

_____

What things in your life are the hardest for you to release to God?

_____

_____

_____

_____

How might believing that God owns it all affect the way you handle money and possessions on a practical level?

_____

_____

_____

_____

_____

Understanding intellectually that God owns it all is one thing; making that a living reality in your life is another. Meditating on God's blessings can help move that truth from your head to your heart and out through your hands.

When was the last time you stopped and really took a good account of God's blessings? If it's been more than a few months, why don't you stop right now and write down some of God's blessings in your life.

_____

_____

_____

_____

_____

It is virtually a universal truth that those who believe that God owns it all are generous and those who don't are not. If you're hiding behind excuses not to give, could it be because you *really* don't believe God owns it all?

If that's true of you, what are the real reasons why your fist is gripped so tightly around your finances?

_____

_____

_____

_____

_____

What do you think you can do to help loosen your grip?

_____

_____

_____

_____

_____

Perhaps you're fully convinced that God does own it all, and you're committed to stewardship. Perhaps you already give generously. But do you keep accounts of how your money is being spent when you give it?

What benchmarks must a ministry and/or organization meet before you will support it?

_____

_____

_____

_____

_____

Think about the ministries and/or organizations you support financially. Are they currently meeting those benchmarks? If not, what should you do about that?

_____

_____

_____

The poet Martha Snell Nicholson understood that God owned all her treasures. And she was willing to give them all up if He wanted them back. She lived open-handedly.

> One by one He took them from me,
> All the things I valued most,
> Until I was empty-handed;
> Every glittering toy was lost.

> And I walked earth's highways,
>   grieving,
> In my rags and poverty.
> Till I heard His voice inviting,
> "Lift those empty hands to Me!"

> So I held my hands toward Heaven,
> And He filled them with a store
> Of His own transcendent riches
> Till they could contain no more.

> And at last I comprehended
> With my stupid mind and dull,
> That God COULD not pour His riches
> Into hands already full! [6]

Trust Him. Let it go. You've been given one main task when it comes to possessions: to be a good steward of what He has entrusted to you. Nothing less. Nothing more. Remember, God owns it all already.

My Questions and Thoughts

Chapter 3

Sacrifice: Personal and Financial

In early January 1958, I was in a U.S. Marine staging regiment back at Camp Pendleton, preparing to ship out. I had a negative attitude toward life in general and toward God in particular. To be honest, I was borderline bitter. Why on earth would He have allowed this to happen? I was convinced I would never smile again.

Rather than hang out in the barracks that final weekend in the States, I decided to take a bus to Pasadena to visit my older brother, Orville, and his wife, Erma Jean. Our time together sped by quickly, and soon I needed to catch the bus back to Camp Pendleton. Just before my brother said good-bye, he handed me a book and told me, "You'll never be the same after you read this." I had no intention of even opening it. I shrugged and mumbled an insincere, "Thanks," as I got on the bus. It was a rainy, cold night. I blinked through tears of loneliness and self-pity as I sat staring out the window. I couldn't even pray. A hard rain hammered against the oversized bus window. My world had collapsed.

Then for some unexplainable reason, I decided to dig into my bag and pull out the book Orville had given me. I flipped on the tiny light above my head as my eyes gazed across the title: *Through Gates of Splendor*. I thought I recognized those words as being from one of the hymns I had sung in church. I opened the book and soon discovered that it was the true account of how five young men had been murdered—really, martyred—by a small tribe of Auca Indians in the Ecuadorian jungle.

The painfully raw and realistic pictures in the book held my attention. One was a tragic scene: the body of one of the missionaries, speared to death and left floating downriver. That did it! I was hooked. I decided that maybe it wouldn't hurt to glance over a chapter or two, if for no other reason than to get my mind off myself.

Seven hours later I finished the last page. I was back at the barracks, sitting on the floor under the only light that stayed on all night. It was just before dawn. I remember it as if it were yesterday. All alone, I laid the book aside, put my head in my hands, and sobbed audibly. Sitting there on that concrete floor, I realized I had just spent all night enraptured by the story of five brave young men whose hearts beat for Christ. Their passion was to win that tribe of Aucas for the singular purpose of introducing each one of them to the Lord Jesus, who had died for their sins. Their ultimate hope in life was not self-centered. On the contrary, it was Christ-centered. Here were five young men fairly near my own age at the time, whose passion for Him was intense—driven by the hope that those in that dangerous tribe might come to know and love Jesus and thereby gain the assurance of forgiveness, secure their eternal life in heaven, and discover His transforming power.

I found myself rebuked. There I was, preoccupied by self-pity because things hadn't gone as I had expected. And here were a few men who had sacrificed their entire lives for a cause that made my situation pale into insignificance. The contrast was embarrassingly real! As one of the men had written so eloquently in his personal journal, "He is no fool who gives what he cannot keep to gain that which he cannot lose." [1]

I cannot describe the change that swept over me as I watched the morning sun break through the windows. My depression had slowly lifted during that night—it never returned. Beginning that morning and throughout the seventeen days aboard the troopship across the Pacific, my whole attitude toward life began transforming. God used this example of selflessness—the sacrifice of those men—to teach me the value of caring more about others than myself. He taught me so many lessons regarding trusting instead of fearing and worrying, seeing His hand at work in difficulties instead of always asking why.

I became a changed man. In the months that followed, that change in perspective made all the difference in how I viewed life. It still does!

Candidly, I am convinced I am in the Lord's work today because I read Elisabeth Elliot's book on the darkest night of my life up to that point. God used her words to touch my soul and reach my heart with His calling to ministry, a vocation fueled by the discipline of sacrifice.

God will occasionally ask some of His own to suffer death for the sake of Christ, but that is not the sacrifice He wants from most of us. He desires that we offer ourselves as nothing less than living sacrifices. You read that correctly. Each one of us is called to become a "living sacrifice."

Those are the words Paul used in his letter to his Christian friends in Rome. In Romans 12:1, we find Paul on his knees before us, begging, "I plead with you" (NLT). Why beg? Because what he was asking for doesn't come naturally or easily or automatically. When people sacrifice, they're usually not doing it on a whim. Sacrifice hurts. Sacrifice works against our natural inclinations to keep a tight hold on our possessions and creature comforts. And we come hardwired with the instinct to watch out for ourselves, to guard against risk, and to preserve our own lives at any cost.

The word Paul used in Romans 12:1, rendered "sacrifice," is the Greek term *thysia*. Interestingly, he used it sparingly—just a handful of times in all of his letters. That says to me that it was not a term he tossed around loosely or lightly, so we should sit up and pay attention whenever we see it. *Thysia* is the same word we find in the book of Hebrews, referring to the Old Testament temple sacrifices, looking toward what Jesus would one day do on the cross.

In Ephesians 5:1–2, Paul called for us to be like Christ, and Paul defined the kind of sacrifice we are to make of ourselves: "Therefore be imitators of God, as beloved children; and walk in love, just as Christ also loved you and gave Himself up for us, an offering and a sacrifice to God as a fragrant aroma."

In that sentence, two significant ideas are placed side by side: offering and sacrifice, *prosphora* and *thysia*. Both picture someone giving up something. In each case, the giver no longer has something that is valuable in his or her possession. But there is a slight distinction, a subtle difference that makes all the difference. An offering is a sacrifice with an added element: choice.

An offering is a voluntary act. Christ made a conscious choice to offer Himself as an atoning sacrifice so that He might have us. We are to make that same choice for the sake of having Him in a more intimate way. Not to earn His pleasure or blessing, but as a means of deeply coming to know Him.

The exercise of sacrifice begins small. As we consistently carry it out, it becomes habitual. To cultivate the discipline of sacrifice, we must apply it in at least three realms of our lives: personal, relational, and material.

Personal Sacrifice

In Matthew 6, we find a record of the day when Jesus delivered His Sermon on the Mount to His friends and followers. He came on rather strong when He discussed material wealth and things that have price tags. (It's good to remember that everything costs something.) As you read the words He spoke to them, you will not see the term *sacrifice*. Keep the word in the back of your mind, however, as you read.

> "Do not store up for yourselves treasures on earth, where moth and rust destroy, and where thieves break in and steal. But store up for yourselves treasures in heaven, where neither moth nor rust destroys, and where thieves do not break in or steal; for where your treasure is, there your heart will be also.

> "The eye is the lamp of the body; so then if your eye is clear, your whole body will be full of light. But if your eye is bad, your whole body will be full of darkness. If then the light that is in you is darkness, how great is the darkness!

> "No one can serve two masters; for either he will hate the one and love the other, or he will be devoted to one and despise the other. You cannot serve God and wealth.

"For this reason I say to you, do not be worried about your life, as to what you will eat or what you will drink; nor for your body, as to what you will put on. Is not life more than food, and the body more than clothing? Look at the birds of the air, that they do not sow, nor reap nor gather into barns, and yet your heavenly Father feeds them. Are you not worth much more than they? And who of you by being worried can add a single hour to his life? And why are you worried about clothing? Observe how the lilies of the field grow; they do not toil nor do they spin, yet I say to you that not even Solomon in all his glory clothed himself like one of these. But if God so clothes the grass of the field, which is alive today and tomorrow is thrown into the furnace, will He not much more clothe you? You of little faith! Do not worry then, saying, 'What will we eat?' or 'What will we drink?' or 'What will we wear for clothing?' For the Gentiles eagerly seek all these things; for your heavenly Father knows that you need all these things. But seek first His kingdom and His righteous-ness, and all these things will be added to you." (Matthew 6:19–33)

I find at least two points of a sermon in Jesus's words. The first is on hoarding—the greedy grappling for more and more stuff. Complicating life with bet-ter, larger, more expensive, more extravagant things that bind us to mandatory service to maintain them. Anytime you hear a sermon on this passage, that's what the preacher usually goes for. It's a valid focus, and I will address financial sacrifice later. However, any sermon based on Jesus's words that only condemns materialism is but half a sermon.

Being the master communicator, Jesus used word pictures that even a little child could understand. A little moth that can eat a garment. A bit of rust that can ultimately destroy a piece of steel. I love His sense of humor displayed in the scene He drew from nature: "Look up in the air. Look at those birds. They don't sow. They don't reap. They don't store food in barns" (see Matthew 6:26).

Personal sacrifice begins with a choice: who will we trust to meet our needs? We naturally serve what we trust. Hoarding wealth is a sure sign that a person trusts things instead of God.

I mentioned my older brother, Orville, at the beginning of this chapter. He was a missionary for more than thirty years in Buenos Aires. Just before that, he did some short-term mission work in Mexico and came north to gather his wife, Erma Jean, and the kids for the long trip down into the heart of South America.

Before leaving, they stopped for a quick visit with our parents. Now, you have to appreciate the kind of man my father was. Look up the word *responsible* in the dictionary, and his picture is there! To him, risks are for those who fail to plan. Responsible people leave nothing to chance. As far as he was concerned, faith is something you exercise when your three backup plans fall through and you have run out of all other options. My father was a believer, but he never understood the life of faith. Not really.

My brother, on the other hand, was stimulated by faith. He has lived his entire adult life on the raw edge of faith. To him, life doesn't get exciting until only God can get us through some specific challenge. That drove Dad nuts!

After a great supper of good ol' collard greens and cornbread, onions, and red beans, my mother and sister went into the kitchen, leaving my father at one end of the table, Orville at the other, and me sitting on one side. Then it started.

"Son, how much money do you have for your long trip?"

"Oh, Dad, don't worry about it. We're gonna be fine."

Before he could change the subject, my father pressed the issue. "Son, how much money do you have in your wallet?"

Orville smiled as he said, "I don't have any money in my wallet."

I sat silent, watching this verbal tennis match.

"How much money do you have? You're gettin' ready to go down to South America! How much money you got?"

With that, my brother dug into his pocket, pulled out a quarter, set it on its edge on his end of the table, then gave it a careful thump. It slowly rolled past me all the way to my father's end of the table and fell into his hand. Dad said, "That is all you've got?"

Orville broke into an even bigger smile and said, "Yeah. *Isn't that exciting!*"

That was not the word my father had in mind at the moment. After a heavy sigh and a very brief pause, Dad shook his head and said, "Orville, I just don't understand you."

My brother grew serious. Looking Dad in the eyes, he answered, "No, Dad, you never have."

I don't know how Orville actually made the trip or how he and Erma Jean took care of all their little kids, but they never went hungry. And they served in Buenos Aires and other parts of South America for more than three decades. My father was a man who emerged through the Great Depression, lived in fear of poverty his whole life, and never experienced the joy of trusting God. Regardless, the possibility of adventure made my brother smile so big that day.

The point of Jesus's sermon was not to say that having nice things is wrong. Read the passage again and look for anything that would suggest that He wanted people to be poor. Whether or not we own nice things, He wants to be sure that we aren't owned by them! As soon as something begins to feel just a little too crucial to our happiness or safety, it's time to apply the discipline of sacrifice.

When was the last time you just gave something away? I mean something very nice. Something that has meant a lot to you. It probably wasn't easy. Sacrifice doesn't come naturally. It's a discipline that requires faith—a trust that the Almighty will look after your needs in ways that you will never see until you allow Him the opportunity.

Dallas Willard explained it much better than I:

> The discipline of sacrifice is one in
> which we forsake the security of
> meeting our needs with what is in our
> hands. It is total abandonment to God, a
> stepping into the darkened abyss in the
> faith and hope that God will bear
> us up. . . .
>
> The cautious faith that never saws
> off a limb on which it is sitting never
> learns that unattached limbs may find
> strange, unaccountable ways of not
> falling.[2]

I wonder how much better we would know our God if we didn't make such a good living. I would be willing to wager that we don't have intimacy with the Almighty because we haven't given enough away. We don't really trust our God sufficiently. To exercise the spiritual discipline of sacrifice, start cultivating generosity.

Relational Sacrifice

In Genesis 22, God had told Abraham that he would be the father of a great nation, a people who would inhabit the land of promise and worship the one true God. All of God's promises to Abraham rested in this one son. How easy for Isaac to become virtually everything to his father! One evening the Lord stepped into Abraham's world: "Take now your son, your only son, whom you love, Isaac, and go to the land of Moriah, and offer him there as a burnt offering on one of the mountains of which I will tell you" (Genesis 22:2).

I'm convinced that Abraham spent a restless night, if not in anguish, at least in soul-searching prayer. Let's face it: Abraham was a hero of faith, but we dare not turn him into a superhero. He was just a man. Imagine how you would feel if you were asked to take the life of your child. Just like you or me, Abraham had to evaluate his priorities and check his faith. After all, God didn't stutter. His voice was clear. Abraham had unmistakable orders from the Lord: "Sacrifice your son."

While I'm sure Abraham didn't sleep at all that night, we are told that he wasted no time obeying:

> So Abraham rose early in the morning and saddled his donkey, and took two of his young men with him and Isaac his son; and he split wood for the burnt offering, and arose and went to the place of which God had told him. On the third day Abraham raised his eyes and saw the place from a distance. Abraham said to his young men, "Stay here with the donkey, and I and the lad will go over there; and we will worship and return to you." (Genesis 22:3–5)

Don't hurry past how Abraham explained his plan to his servants. "We will go." And then? "We will worship." What a great perspective! Sacrifice is worship. Notice also, "*and* return to you." In the Hebrew, Abraham was specific in his use of the plural. He didn't say, "*We* will go worship, and *I* will return to you." We cannot know for sure what he was thinking. He knew that he would have to kill Isaac, but he also knew that God would keep His promises—the promises that rested in Isaac. Hebrews 11:17–19 clearly states that

Abraham knew God could raise Isaac from the dead once he sacrificed Isaac's life on the altar. Whatever Abraham's thinking, he obeyed:

> Abraham took the wood of the burnt
> offering and laid it on Isaac his son,
> and he took in his hand the fire and
> the knife. So the two of them walked
> on together. Isaac spoke to Abraham
> his father and said, "My father!" And he
> said, "Here I am, my son." And he said,
> "Behold, the fire and the wood,
> but where is the lamb for the burnt
> offering?" (Genesis 22:6–7)

Isaac had been mentored in the sacrifices. He had helped his father prepare sacrifices before. He saw the torch and the firewood but saw no animal. Abraham was so wise. Now he mentored his son in faith:

> Abraham said, "God will provide for
> Himself the lamb for the burnt offering,
> my son." So the two of them walked on
> together. (22:8)

The whole story turns on trust. There was no argument, there was no further questioning, and the boy trusted his dad. Even better, the dad was confident in his God:

> Then they came to the place of which
> God had told him; and Abraham built
> the altar there and arranged the wood,
> and bound his son Isaac and laid him
> on the altar, on top of the wood.
> Abraham stretched out his hand and
> took the knife to slay his son. But the
> angel of the LORD called to him from

heaven and said, "Abraham, Abraham!"
And he said, "Here I am." He said, "Do
not stretch out your hand against the
lad, and do nothing to him; for now I
know that you fear God, since you have
not withheld your son, your only son,
from Me." (Genesis 22:9–12)

God took Abraham all the way to the edge of his
relationship with his son. This faithful servant said
by his actions, "Lord, You're more to me than any
relationship ever will be. If You tell me to put the most
important person in the world to me on an altar, I'll
sacrifice him."

A.W. Tozer wrote about this struggle in his fine
book *The Pursuit of God*:

We are often hindered from giving up
our treasures to the Lord out of fear
for their safety. This is especially true
when those treasures are loved relatives
and friends. But we need have no such
fears. Our Lord came not to destroy but
to save. Everything is safe which we
commit to Him, and nothing is really
safe which is not so committed.[3]

ℱinancial Ṣacrifice

Personal sacrifice overcomes a love for self that may
be nurtured by any number of things, material wealth
being only one of them. Financial sacrifice overcomes a
love for money and possessions. In my own experience,
this is probably the easiest of the three to address. When
one adequately deals with personal sacrifice and relational sacrifice, financial sacrifices naturally follow. By

the time one has worked through the issues of personal treasures and idolatrous relationships, money becomes so insignificant!

Paul's letter to the church in Philippi—a letter from an itinerant preacher to a new and growing church—is a very sweet note overflowing with joy and thanksgiving. These brothers and sisters loved Paul and believed in his ministry, and they lived to give. Overflowing with feelings of gratitude, Paul wrote to them:

> You yourselves also know, Philippians,
> that at the first preaching of the gospel,
> after I left Macedonia, no church shared
> with me in the matter of giving and
> receiving but you alone; for even in
> Thessalonica you sent a gift more than
> once for my needs. Not that I seek the
> gift itself, but I seek for the profit which
> increases to your account. But I have
> received everything in full and have
> an abundance; I am amply supplied,
> having received from Epaphroditus
> what you have sent, a fragrant aroma,
> an acceptable sacrifice, well-pleasing to
> God. (Philippians 4:15–18)

From verse 15, we discover that this church was *the only one* to give. Verse 16 tells us that they gave *repeatedly.* We know from verse 18 that they gave *recently* and *generously.* Paul put his finger on the word that best describes such liberal giving on the part of the Philippians: *sacrifice.*

Notice also the follow-up promise Paul set forth in verse 19: "And my God will supply all your needs according to His riches in glory in Christ Jesus."

Their part was repeated generosity. God's part was abundantly supplying their need.

The great fear in financial sacrifice is that we might run out of provisions. We're tempted to think that giving them away will only bring the poverty sooner. Thankfully, as with relationships, God will provide. He is infinite in His resources and in His creativity. He never runs dry or shy of ideas.

Regrettably, many people, both within the church and without, honestly feel money is "filthy lucre," so we are better off not even mentioning it. I have actually heard laymen bragging that their minister has never once talked about money during the years he has been their pastor. While I have serious concerns about such silence, I understand how that could happen. I, too, tend to shy away from the subject.

What Makes Us So Dreadfully Defensive?

Having been engaged in ministry for about four decades, I can remember times when I could almost hear the groans and feel the sighs as I announced that I'd be speaking on giving that particular Sunday. Why do we feel that way? I think it is a lot like the groans and sighs we release in mid-October when the stores drag out the plastic trees and put Santa Claus in the windows. Three specific analogies come to mind.

First, *it seems terribly repetitive.* The subject of giving is seldom approached creatively, and then when it is addressed, the comments are usually overstated and punctuated with guilt-giving remarks. Most often the congregation is not instructed as much as they are exhorted and exploited. Furthermore, there is neither subtlety nor much humor employed—only large helpings of hardcore facts mixed with a pinch of panic "because giving has dropped off." It doesn't take a Ph.D. from Yale to sense the objective during the first five minutes: *Give More!* Same song, ninth verse. The repetitive cycle gets monotonous.

Second, *the whole thing has been commercialized.* Because grace has been separated from giving, greed has come in like the proverbial flood. Mr. and Mrs. Average Christian are punchy, suspicious, and resentful—sometimes for good reason. During the latter half of the twentieth century, all of us were embarrassed, weren't we? We saw shameful examples of greed employed in the name of religion. Unbelievable techniques were used to wrench money from the public's pockets, and we've gotten fed up with the gimmicks. Everybody wants more, not just religious folks. Enough is never enough.

Third, *there always seems to be a hidden agenda.* Just as merchants don't go to a lot of extra expense and trouble getting their stores ready for Christmas simply for the fun of it, neither do most ministers speak on financial stewardship because it is a fun subject. The bottom line is usually uppermost. The emphasis is seldom on the charming joy of grace-oriented giving but rather on the obligation and responsibility to give "whether you like it or not."

This is an appropriate time for me to mention a couple of things, just to set the record straight. How and why we give is of far greater significance to God than what we give. Attitude and motive are always more important than amount. Furthermore, once a person cultivates a taste for grace in giving, the amount becomes virtually immaterial. When those age-old grace killers—namely guilt and manipulation—are not used as leverage, the heart responds in generosity. Giving at that point becomes wonderfully addictive.

What Makes Giving So Wonderfully Addictive?

Grace can liberate you to become a model of unusual and consistent generosity, all the while filling you with inexpressible joy. No, this is not some ideal reserved for a chosen few; this is reality for all of God's people to claim.

Now is the right moment to step into the time tunnel and return to the first century. The original church in Jerusalem had fallen on hard times. Unable to pull itself out of a financial slump, thanks to the depressed economy in Judea and other nearby regions, those early believers were facing a bleak and barren future.

As is often the case in our own times, while one part of the world was suffering great need, another was flourishing. The Greeks in Corinth were doing quite well, which prompted Paul to urge them to give financial assistance to their fellow Christians in Jerusalem. His words to the Corinthian believers regarding this need are recorded in 2 Corinthians 8 and 9, two of the finest chapters in the entire Bible on grace giving.

At the beginning of his charge, he mentioned the generosity of the struggling churches in Macedonia who gave during days of affliction. In spite of their own poverty and with great joy, they took delight in giving to those in need. Paul urged the Corinthians to follow the example they set. Those words of background information will help you understand the apostle's opening remarks:

Now, brethren, we wish to make known
to you the grace of God which has been
given in the churches of Macedonia,
that in a great ordeal of affliction
their abundance of joy and their deep
poverty overflowed in the wealth of
their liberality. For I testify that according to their ability, and beyond their
ability, they gave of their own accord,
begging us with much urging for the
favor of participation in the support
of the saints, and this, not as we had
expected, but they first gave themselves
to the Lord and to us by the will of God.
(2 Corinthians 8:1–5)

Paul admitted that he was surprised. He stated
that what the Macedonians gave was "not as we had
expected." Of greater importance, their gifts did not
originate in their purses and wallets. No, "they first
gave *themselves* to the Lord" (emphasis added), and then
they gave their money. Grace giving begins in the heart.
Grace-oriented generosity is the overflow of a liberated
heart. This assures us that it has nothing to do with
one's investment portfolio or monthly salary. Whether
Macedonian or Corinthian, American or Canadian,
Asian or Australian, the challenge is the same: first and
foremost, we are to give ourselves to the Lord. When we
do, our treasure will follow the leading of our heart.

Returning to my earlier question, what is it that
makes all this so addictive?

First, *it helps us keep a healthy balance.* "But just as
you abound in everything, in faith and utterance and
knowledge and in all earnestness and in the love we

inspired in you, see that you abound in this gracious work also" (2 Corinthians 8:7).

In many a church there is faith; there is good teaching ("utterance"), a working knowledge of the Christian life; there is zeal, spiritual passion, and a great deal of love . . . but generosity? A superabundant willingness to give? Often that is the one ingredient conspicuous by its absence. How easy to take, to be blessed, instructed, encouraged, exhorted, affirmed, and strengthened—all those things received in abundance—yet fail to balance the receiving with our giving.

Did you notice how Paul referred to financial support? He called it "this gracious work," and he exhorted us to "abound" in it. The Christian life takes on a healthy balance when our taking in and giving out stay in step. You and I feel closer to the Savior because that is what He did—He gave. "For you know the grace of our Lord Jesus Christ, that though He was rich, yet for your sake He became poor, so that you through His poverty might become rich" (8:9).

The second reason that giving is addictive is that *in giving, we model the same grace of Jesus Christ*. I am impressed that the verse of Scripture doesn't say, "For you know the obligation of the Lord Jesus Christ" or "You know the sense of duty," though that is true. It was a duty that He come to earth. But Paul didn't write, "You know the requirement" or "You know the sacrifice." No, he mentioned only the grace. When our Lord Jesus left heaven, He didn't leave gritting His teeth and clenching His fists, shouting, "Okay . . . *Okay!*" It wasn't obligation—it was grace that motivated Him to come. It was grace within Him that brought Him to Bethlehem as a little baby. It was grace within Him that allowed

His hands and feet to be pierced with nails and grace within Him to say, "Father, forgive them; for they do not know what they are doing" (Luke 23:34). When you give knowing there will be no gift in return, you have modeled the purest form of the grace of the Lord Jesus Christ. It will help if you think about giving in that way.

Let me mention a third reason that generosity based on grace is so addictive: *you can't help but be generous when grace consumes you.* "Now this I say, he who sows sparingly will also reap sparingly, and he who sows bountifully will also reap bountifully" (2 Corinthians 9:6).

That is an encouraging verse for anyone who fears that giving more will result in "running out." If I read these words correctly, the bountiful sower becomes that kind of reaper. I cannot explain the beauty and the wonder of it all, but this much I know for sure: we cannot outgive our God.

What Makes Giving with Grace So Attractive?

Beginning in 2 Corinthians 9:6, through the end of the chapter, I discover four things that make grace so attractive, not just at the Christmas season but all through the year. In verse 7, we are told: "Each one must do just as he has purposed in his heart."

Here is the first reason grace is so attractive: *grace individualizes the gift.* When you give by grace, you give individually. You give proportionately to your own income. You have needs, and you have an income to meet those needs. That combination is unlike anyone else's on earth. You are an individual. When you give on that basis, your gift is an individual kind of gift. We are not all shoved into a tank, blended together, then "required" to give exactly 10 percent. (Though if everyone gave 10 percent, we would have such an enormous surplus in God's work we would not know what to do with the extra—but I'm sure we'd quickly find out.) It is much more individualized than that. Grace, remember, brings variety and spontaneity.

If you are married, how about regularly discussing your giving plans with your mate? Or if you are single and you have a job where your salary is increasing and you respect your parents and their giving habits, how about talking over with them a game plan for giving during the next year? By discussing it, you can discover ways to individualize your style of giving. Paul put it this way: "Each *one* must do *just* as he has purposed in his heart" (2 Corinthians 9:7, emphasis added).

You know our problem? Most folks don't "purpose"; they don't plan; they impulsively react. But God says, "Each one must do just as he has purposed in his heart." Think of how carefully you would plan a room addition. You leave nothing to chance, making certain not to miss one detail, one electrical socket in your planning, one window placement, or one place where you will or will not use carpet. You purpose and plan exactly how you want to add on to the house. I challenge you to do the same with your giving. Give grace a chance! Start with planning, praying, and thinking it through. Determine the amount and where your gift will go and when, and then release it with joy.

The second reason grace is so attractive: *grace makes the action joyfully spontaneous*: "Not grudgingly or under compulsion, for God loves a cheerful giver" (9:7).

I never have been able to understand why everyone in the church looks so serious during the offering. Wouldn't it be great if when the offering plates are passed in church next Sunday, instead of grim looks, stoic silence, and soft organ music you hear laughter? I can just imagine: "Can you believe we're doing this?" "Put it in the plate, honey. Isn't this great? Put it in!" . . . followed by little ripples of laughter and applause across the place of worship. Wonderful! Why not? Deep within the heart there is an absence of any compulsion, only spontaneous laughter. The word *cheerful* is literally a Greek term from which we get the word *hilarious*. "God loves a *hilarious* giver."

I have said it all through my ministry, and I'll repeat it again: if your giving isn't done with hilarity, don't bother. Giving is not for the unbeliever or for those who are grim and resentful. Such giving will not be blessed. The best kind of giving has no strings attached.

Now for a third reason grace is so attractive: *grace enables us to link up with God's supply line.* Look at verse 8: "And God is able to make all grace abound to you, so that always having all sufficiency in everything, you may have an abundance for every good deed." When we possess an attitude of grace, we give. We give ourselves. We give from what we earn. And He, in turn, gives back in various ways, not matching gift for gift, but in an abundance of ways, He goes beyond.

A fourth reason grace is so attractive: *grace leads to incomparable results.*

> Because of the proof given by this
> ministry, they will glorify God for your
> obedience to your confession of the
> gospel of Christ, and for the liberality

of your contribution to them and to
all, while they also, by prayer on your
behalf, yearn for you because of the
surpassing grace of God in you.
(2 Corinthians 9:13–14)

As I read these verses, I find at least three results I
would call "incomparable":

1. Others give God the glory.

2. They learn, by example, to be generous.

3. The relationship transcends any gift we give.

Allow me one final bit of counsel: once you begin
to give on the basis of grace, do so *confidentially*. In
plain English, keep your mouth closed. Keep the extent
of your giving to yourself. Ideally, do so anonymously.
And He who rewards in secret will fulfill His part of the
bargain.

The "apostle of grace" concluded this lengthy
section on giving by announcing, "Thanks be to God
for His indescribable gift!" (9:15). Paul had a pretty good
vocabulary, but when he attempted to describe God's gift
of Christ, he ran out of Greek words. He simply couldn't
find a word for it, so he admitted it is *indescribable*.

Elisabeth Elliot's book introduced me to the discipline of sacrifice that dark, damp night when everything
seemed so bleak. I began a journey that would teach me
what it meant to be a living sacrifice. In my naiveté, I
had assumed that being a living sacrifice meant having
a willingness to lay down my life for Christ in one grand
gesture, much as those five missionaries had done. As
a marine, I had already considered the possibility of
dying for my country. I felt sure I would die for Christ
if circumstances demanded it. But Elisabeth Elliot's

book showed me so much more. She wrote in the 1958 epilogue of *Through Gates of Splendor*:

> We know that it was no accident. God performs all things according to the counsel of His own will. The real issues at stake on January 8, 1956, were very far greater than those which immediately involved five young men and their families, or this small tribe of naked "savages." Letters from many countries have told of God's dealings with hundreds of men and women, through the example of five who believed literally that "the world passeth away, and the lust thereof: but he that doeth the will of God abideth for ever."[4]

These men didn't go on a suicide mission. Their goal was not to die. Their death was the result of living a habitual life of sacrifice to Christ. Their precious lives ended in tragedy near a river in the Ecuadorian interior in the early days of 1956. They were no fools. They were heroes of the life of faith. Their deaths taught me what it meant to live. Really live.

God will not likely expect you to surrender your life all at once as these men did. Instead, He patiently waits for you to sacrifice yourself in small amounts, one decision at a time, one day at a time, so that you might enjoy an ever-increasing intimacy with Him. And this deepening intimacy with Him will inevitably make you more like Christ.

My Questions and Thoughts

My Questions and Thoughts

_____

_____

_____

_____

_____

_____

_____

_____

_____

_____

_____

_____

_____

_____

_____

_____

_____

_____

_____

_____

_____

_____

_____

Chapter 4

Love, Loans . . . and the Money Crunch

You Are Here

Making sense of dollars and cents is a funda-
mental requirement for everyone who wants
to make something out of his or her life. At the very
least, all of us must learn how to balance a checkbook
and live in such a way that our yearnings don't get ahead
of our earnings. A sure method to ensure that we live
within our means is to have a financial plan. This
timeless wisdom even caught the attention of Jesus.

> Is there anyone here who, planning
> to build a new house, doesn't first sit
> down and figure the cost so you'll know
> if you can complete it? If you only get
> the foundation laid and then run out
> of money, you're going to look pretty
> foolish. Everyone passing by will poke
> fun at you: "He started something he
> couldn't finish." (Luke 14:28–30 MSG)

In the opinion of our Lord, careful money management is not considered an optional luxury; it is an
essential ingredient in the lives of those who follow
Him. But what if we fail to plan or if something unfore-
seen occurs and we find ourselves with more month at
the end of our paychecks? What do we do then?

Discovering the Way

For the wise, no lesson is learned with more speed and thoroughness than the lessons taught in the schoolroom of economic stress. For the fool . . . well, the fool will never learn, whether in the schoolroom of financial ruin or on the playground of prosperity. The fool will squander whatever prosperity comes his or her way and will become ruined by staying in the deep pit of debt. It's for good reason that the oft-quoted maxim, "A fool and his money are soon parted," has become a cliché.

Samuel Johnson was no fool. He learned and taught the lesson that debt is a destroyer.

> Do not accustom yourself to consider
> debt only as an inconvenience; you will
> find it a calamity. Poverty takes away
> so many means of doing good, and
> produces so much inability to resist evil,
> both natural and moral, that it is by all
> virtuous means to be avoided.[1]

What is your honest opinion or attitude toward debt?

_____

_____

_____

_____

_____

Shakespeare advised, "Neither a borrower nor a lender be."[2] What do you think about Christians becoming creditors or debtors?

_____

_____

_____

_____

_____

Have you found yourself in financial difficulties? What was the cause of your financial troubles (failure to plan, spending more than you earn, the failure of a business, a sudden or severe illness with medical bills)? What lesson(s) did you learn?

_____

_____

_____

_____

_____

_____

A Historical Situation

Nehemiah was the furthest thing from foolish. Supervising the rebuilding of the walls around Jerusalem after Nebuchadnezzar and his Babylonian army had destroyed the city seventy years earlier was a task no fool could have skillfully managed. And Nehemiah had done a masterful job in planning, organizing, and leading the effort. But now he faced a new challenge—an economic challenge.

For many years, the Jews of Nehemiah's time had been gradually returning from exile in Babylon to live again in Jerusalem. But, though the people were free, Jerusalem's economy had not recovered after being devastated by the Babylonians. All business, trade, and farming had been either ruined or disrupted. Now, under a triple threat, the struggling economy opened a fragile fault line that ran through the center of Israel's economic structure into the people's pocketbooks. Such a fissure could easily split open if the wrong kinds of pressures were applied. And as those pressures began to build, Israel's families began to crumble. Their cooperative will to complete the task of rebuilding was breaking apart, and people began to blame one another in a potentially disastrous upheaval.

 Read Nehemiah 5:1–5.

Whether balancing the family checkbook or the nation's budget, everyone has to cope with money problems and the personal issues that inevitably arise. In fact, financial problems are one of the greatest sources of stress in a marriage, ministry, or business.

For Nehemiah, a money crunch led to a workers' strike. The "Wall Builder's Union" probably didn't picket the work site with signs and try to prevent others from "crossing the line," but they stopped working and started complaining about their conditions (Nehemiah 5:1–2).

Identify the three complaints the people lodged with Nehemiah in 5:3–5.

Verse 3: _____

Verse 4: _____

Verse 5: _____

Three Reasons for the Money Crunch

The first money crunch came as a result of a *famine* (Nehemiah 5:3). For seventy years, while the Jews were in exile in Babylon, the land surrounding the city of Jerusalem had lain fallow—it hadn't been cultivated. Now, with an influx of people, there weren't enough productive crops to sustain everyone, a situation exacerbated by the famine. In order to survive and buy food, the people were forced to mortgage their property.

The second crunch came from the heavy *taxes* imposed by King Artaxerxes (5:4). Artaxerxes ruled most of the known world at the time and had armies spread out over the empire to ensure that he continued to rule. But these armies didn't fight for free. He taxed everyone living in his kingdom, including the Jewish laborers trying to rebuild Jerusalem's wall. To pay the heavy burden of Artaxerxes's taxes—and the corrupt tax collectors who skimmed off the top—the people had to borrow money.

The third money crunch was more subtle: some of the wealthier Jews were charging exorbitant interest rates on borrowed money, a practice known as *usury* (5:5). In ancient times, the custom of usury involved indentured servitude until the debt was paid off. A man who borrowed money at an inappropriately high interest rate would exchange labor for enough money to pay off his debts, becoming a slave to his creditor for a certain period of time until that debt was also paid. But often creditors charged so much interest that the borrower could never end his term of service or the creditor would repossess the borrower's land and crops or even take his children as slaves in lieu of payment.

This triple pressure not only put a crunch on the people's morale, causing a halt on the work on the wall, it also threatened to shake apart the fragile Jewish society in Jerusalem. Nehemiah had to act—and act quickly.

Sometimes we respond to financial problems by burying our heads in the sand, hoping these problems will just go away. When was the last time you sized up your own financial responsibilities? If you had to give an on-the-spot report of the financial standing of your family, ministry, or business, would you have the information to do so? Why, or why not?

_____

_____

_____

_____

_____

If you answered no above, whom would you need to talk with or what would you need to do to get the appropriate information?

_____

_____

_____

What are the risks of not knowing the facts?

_____

_____

_____

_____

_____

What do you think is the primary root of most financial problems people face today (lack of adequate compensation, unfair treatment or competition, debt, or something else)? Defend your answer with specific examples.

_____

_____

_____

_____

_____

_____

Do you see any of these sources of financial stress cropping up in the management of your personal finances or the business finances for which you may be responsible? Which sources of stress affect you the most?

_____

_____

_____

_____

_____

The Leader's Reaction

How did Nehemiah respond when he heard about Israel's perilous financial situation? He became angry.

 Read Nehemiah 5:6.

After hearing the people's complaint, Nehemiah "burned with anger."[3] His fury sizzled. He was angry because the people had forgotten the Mosaic Law. God had given the Law to instruct Israel as to how they were to live distinct and God-honoring lives in the midst of a God-blaspheming people. But the Jews refused to follow instructions. And in a foolish twist of irony, the Jews who wanted the walls of Jerusalem rebuilt were the same Jews who were charging usury, preventing the construction of the walls. What the people needed to do was reread the instructions found in the divine Law.

Rereading the Instructions

The Law of Moses is found primarily in the books of Exodus, Leviticus, and Deuteronomy. And though these instructions were given directly to the ancient people of Israel, twenty-first century Christians would do well to heed principles found in God's financial guidelines.

Read Exodus 22:25 and Deuteronomy 23:19–20. Summarize the appropriate lending practices for God's people.

_____

_____

_____

_____

_____

Read Leviticus 25:35–43. Summarize the appropriate practices regarding slavery.

_____

_____

_____

_____

_____

How had the Israelites disregarded both the letter
and the spirit of these commands?

_____

_____

_____

_____

What were the results of their failure to abide by the
statutes God had given them?

_____

_____

_____

_____

How can you apply the financial principles found in
these passages to modern-day financial pressures?

_____

_____

_____

_____

_____

_____

An examination of the Old Testament law reveals
that it was not wrong to lend money or to charge interest
to non-Jews, but Jews were not to charge interest when
lending money to each other. Also, it was acceptable for
a Jew to render service to a lender in payment of a debt,
but slavery was absolutely prohibited between Jews.
And even if a Jew sold himself to another Jew as a hired
worker, the Law of Moses declared that all workers must
be released in the Year of Jubilee.

According to the Hebrew calendar, every fiftieth year was to be celebrated as the Jubilee year, the "year of liberty" (Ezekiel 46:17). During this year,

> All property . . . which the owner had been obliged to sell through poverty . . . was to revert without payment to its original owner or his lawful heirs. . . . Every Israelite, who through poverty had sold himself to one of his country-men or to a foreigner settled in the land . . . was to go out free with his children.[4]

Failure to follow these simple rules would result in economic and social consequences . . . such as the problems detailed in Nehemiah 5. Given this background, it's no wonder that Nehemiah's first response was righteous anger. If the people had followed the Law of Moses and done what was just and right in the area of finances, these problems would have never erupted.

The Practical Solution

Nehemiah responded to the peoples' complaints with anger, but that doesn't mean he spewed out his anger indiscriminately. Nehemiah was wise enough to channel the heat of his conviction toward the problem, not toward the people. He chose to relieve the financial pressure by realigning the peoples' practices to bring them in line with the Law of Moses.

 Read Nehemiah 5:7–9.

It has been said that "anger may glance into the Breast of a wise Man—but rests only in the Bosom of Fools."[5] Anger never found a home in Nehemiah's heart because he was no fool. In his anger, Nehemiah retreated to a quiet place and "consulted" with himself (Nehemiah 5:7). He calmed down and thought through the issue, as well as possible solutions. No doubt, Nehemiah prayed and consulted God's Word. And once he believed he understood God's mind on the issue, he tackled the dilemma head-on, without fear or compromise.

Solving the People's Financial Dilemma

Nehemiah didn't level his ire at all the people but targeted those responsible for the financial meltdown, the nobles and rulers—the rich whose wallets were getting heavier through corruption (Nehemiah 5:6). Nehemiah made three charges against them.

- He accused them of charging outrageous interest on their fellow Jews (5:7).

- He blamed them for allowing permanent slavery of Jewish debtors (5:8).

- He charged them with losing their distinction in the eyes of the surrounding Gentile nations (5:9).

The willful disobedience of these Jewish moneymen brought reproach on the reputation of the Lord from the pagan world around them. Nehemiah exposed them as crooks by shining the interrogator's light of God's Law on their illegal practices. And their reaction proved that they were guilty on all counts: "They were silent and could not find a word to say" (5:8).

 Read Nehemiah 5:10–13.

Shining the light of truth on a soggy ceiling, however, is not enough to fix the leak, whether personal or national. The roof must be repaired. So, Nehemiah proposed some constructive changes that can apply to all situations in which financial wrong has been done.

First, *determine to stop the wrong* (Nehemiah 5:10). Once the conviction of sin pricks the conscience, stop sinning. It's as simple as that! And once the cause of a financial crunch is discovered, stop that practice — immediately.

Second, *make a specific plan to correct the wrong immediately, regardless the sacrifice involved* (5:11). The old cliché is correct: never put off till tomorrow what you can do today. Nehemiah told the shady bankers to give back everything they had taken from the people, "this very day." True repentance for wrong always inspires a desire to provide restitution. Repentance is a sincere desire to reverse, as much as possible, the damage already done — and to do so with haste.

Third, *declare your plans for correction in a promise before God* (5:12). These men were willing to follow God's ways and restore those they had harmed. So Nehemiah called the priests and had the men who had cheated the people swear an oath to follow through with their commitment.

Finally, *realize the seriousness of your vow to God* (5:13). God is not one to be trifled with. A promise is a debt unpaid, and God is a meticulous bookkeeper. The Jews understood this. And just in case they needed a reminder, Nehemiah gave them a dramatic warning: "I also shook out the front of my garment and said, 'Thus may God shake out every man from his house and from his possessions who does not fulfill this promise.'"

All the people who stood watching Nehemiah's speech shouted "Amen" while praising God (5:13).

Starting Your Journey

Finances can cause tremors in many people's lives. Marriages, homes, businesses, and even churches collapse because of shaky money management. And while we can't escape rumblings every now and then, we don't have to crumble under the weight of money matters. Consider these four solid insights as you build a financial foundation that won't buckle under pressure.

First, *God is pleased with the wise handling of our money.* God has left us ample materials in His Word for building solid financial principles into our lives. And not only in the book of Nehemiah—from Genesis to Revelation, the subject of money takes up a great deal of space. In fact, some scholars have shown that the subject of money is spoken of in the New Testament more often than the subjects of both heaven and hell.[6]

Compare Paul's attitude toward money in Philippians 4:11–19 and 2 Corinthians 6:10 with the ruler's attitude in Matthew 19:16–22. Which attitude mirrors your own? Which of your actions and financial decisions support your answer? Give specific examples.

_____

_____

_____

_____

_____

_____

Second, *prolonged personal sin takes a heavy toll on the public work of God.* Technically, the people's finances had nothing to do with the stones and mortar of the construction project. Yet, on the practical side, their sin caused the entire project to grind to a halt.

Reflect on your current financial responsibilities. What are your weaknesses or potential pitfalls? Many of us have "blind spots" when it comes to money management. Consider asking a trusted Christian friend or financial counselor for his or her perspective on how you handle money; record what you learn here.

_____

_____

_____

_____

_____

How could these weaknesses affect the financial goals you're trying to accomplish?

_____

_____

_____

_____

If you're a leader in a business or organization, what can you do to help those under your guidance develop sound financial habits?

_____

_____

_____

_____

How can you teach solid financial principles to your family?

_____

_____

_____

_____

Third, *correcting sin in our lives begins with facing it head-on.* Many of us spend so much time excusing and rationalizing our sin that we muffle the convicting voice of the Holy Spirit. Rather than dodging sinful attitudes about our dealings with money, we need to develop a righteous disgust for such things and actively root them out.

Are you allowing any sinful attitudes about money to go unchecked? Are you struggling with unwise financial decisions in your personal life? What are they? What must you do to acknowledge and confront these issues?

_____

_____

_____

_____

_____

Fourth, *correction is often carried out more effectively when we make a public promise.* Like the Jewish nobles and rulers before the priests, share your commitment to change with someone who knows you well. Confide in an intimate friend or a trusted Bible-study group—people who can encourage you and help solidify your resolve to be more obedient to the Lord with your finances.

Financial accountability is not easy, but it's absolutely necessary. What systems of financial accountability do you currently have in place to protect yourself from making unwise decisions?

_____

_____

_____

_____

_____

Do you need greater accountability in your finances? Name some people you can trust as consultants or confidants as you seek to honor the Lord with your money.

_____

_____

_____

_____

_____

⁂

Money problems and financial stresses can bring businesses, ministries, governments, and families to their knees. Following wise, biblical financial principles may feel like drudgery when so much more urgent work needs to be done. However, the lessons from Nehemiah's experience demonstrate the importance of godly financial accountability. If your finances lie in disarray, _now_ is the time to set them in order.

My Questions and Thoughts

My Questions and Thoughts

_____

_____

_____

_____

_____

_____

_____

_____

_____

_____

_____

_____

_____

_____

_____

_____

_____

_____

_____

_____

_____

_____

_____

_____

_____

_____

How to Begin a Relationship with God

Money is sneaky. It is something all of us need in this life, but if we're not careful, our need for money can quickly and subtly turn into an unhealthy desire for more and more money. When this happens, we no longer own money; it owns us. Money is a benevolent servant but a tyrannical master; it demands exclusive allegiance. Jesus put it this way, "You can't worship two gods at once. Loving one god, you'll end up hating the other. Adoration of one feeds contempt for the other. You can't worship God and Money both" (Matthew 6:24 MSG).

Anyone who bows before the altar of the almighty dollar soon discovers it is a false god, bringing misery instead of true happiness and richness. Only one God can bring true happiness and richness to life—the God who owns it all. His name is Jesus. And He can only be found by walking the path of faith, not Wall Street. The Bible marks the path with four essential truths. If you'd like to meet this God who owns it all, look with me at each marker in detail.

Our Spiritual Condition: Totally Corrupt

The first truth is rather personal. One look in the mirror of Scripture, and our human condition becomes painfully clear:

> "There is none righteous, not even one;
> There is none who understands,
> There is none who seeks for God;
> All have turned aside, together they
>   have become useless;
> There is none who does good,
> There is not even one."
> (Romans 3:10–12)

We are all sinners through and through—totally depraved. Now, that doesn't mean we've committed every atrocity known to humankind. We're not as *bad* as we can be, just as *bad off* as we can be. Sin colors all our thoughts, motives, words, and actions.

If you've been around a while, you likely already believe it. Look around. Everything around us bears the smudge marks of our sinful nature. Despite our best efforts to create a perfect world, crime statistics continue to soar, divorce rates keep climbing, and families keep crumbling.

Something has gone terribly wrong in our society and in ourselves—something deadly. Contrary to how the world would repackage it, "me-first" living doesn't equal rugged individuality and freedom; it equals death. As Paul said in his letter to the Romans, "The wages of sin is death" (Romans 6:23)—our spiritual and physical death that comes from God's righteous judgment of our sin, along with all of the emotional and practical effects of this separation that we experience on a daily basis. This brings us to the second marker: God's character.

God's Character: Infinitely Holy

How can God judge us for a sinful state we were born into? Our total depravity is only half the answer. The other half is God's infinite holiness.

The fact that we know things are not as they should be points us to a standard of goodness beyond ourselves. Our sense of injustice in life on this side of eternity implies a perfect standard of justice beyond our reality. That standard and source is God Himself. And God's standard of holiness contrasts starkly with our sinful condition.

Scripture says that "God is Light, and in Him there is no darkness at all" (1 John 1:5). God is absolutely holy—which creates a problem for us. If He is so pure, how can we who are so impure relate to Him?

Perhaps we could try being better people, try to tilt the balance in favor of our good deeds, or seek out methods for self-improvement. Throughout history, people have attempted to live up to God's standard by keeping the Ten Commandments or living by their own code of ethics. Unfortunately, no one can come close to satisfying the demands of God's law. Romans 3:20 says, "By the works of the Law no flesh will be justified in His sight; for through the Law comes the knowledge of sin."

Our Need: A Substitute

So here we are, sinners by nature and sinners by choice, trying to pull ourselves up by our own bootstraps to attain a relationship with our holy Creator. But every time we try, we fall flat on our faces. We can't live a good enough life to make up for our sin, because God's standard isn't "good enough"—it's *perfection*. And we can't make amends for the offense our sin has created without dying for it.

Who can get us out of this mess?

If someone could live perfectly, honoring God's law, and would bear sin's death penalty for us—in our place—then we would be saved from our predicament. But is there such a person? Thankfully, yes!

Meet your substitute—*Jesus Christ*. He is the One who took death's place for you!

> [God] made [Jesus Christ] who knew no sin to be sin on our behalf, so that we might become the righteousness of God in Him. (2 Corinthians 5:21)

God's Provision: A Savior

God rescued us by sending His Son, Jesus, to die on the cross for our sins (1 John 4:9–10). Jesus was fully human and fully divine (John 1:1, 18), a truth that ensures His understanding of our weaknesses, His power to forgive, and His ability to bridge the gap between God and us (Romans 5:6–11). In short, we are "justified as a gift by His grace through the redemption which is in Christ Jesus" (Romans 3:24). Two words in this verse bear further explanation: *justified* and *redemption*.

Justification is God's act of mercy, in which He declares righteous the believing sinners while we are still in our sinning state. Justification doesn't mean that God *makes* us righteous, so that we never sin again, rather that He *declares* us righteous—much like a judge pardons a guilty criminal. Because Jesus took our sin upon Himself and suffered our judgment on the cross, God forgives our debt and proclaims us PARDONED.

Redemption is Christ's act of paying the complete price to release us from sin's bondage. God sent His Son to bear His wrath for all of our sins—past, present, and future (Romans 3:24–26; 2 Corinthians 5:21). In humble obedience, Christ willingly endured the shame of the cross for our sake (Mark 10:45; Romans 5:6–8; Philippians 2:8). Christ's death satisfied God's righteous demands. He no longer holds our sins against us, because His own Son paid the penalty for them. We are freed from the slave market of sin, never to be enslaved again!

Placing Your Faith in Christ

These four truths describe how God has provided a way to Himself through Jesus Christ. Because the price has been paid in full by God, we must respond to His free gift of eternal life in total faith and confidence in Him to save us. We must step forward into the relationship with God that He has prepared for us—not by doing good works or by being a good person, but by coming to Him just as we are and accepting His justification and redemption by faith.

> For by grace you have been saved
> through faith; and that not of your-
> selves, it is the gift of God; not as a
> result of works, so that no one may
> boast. (Ephesians 2:8–9)

We accept God's gift of salvation simply by placing our faith in Christ alone for the forgiveness of our sins. Would you like to enter a relationship with your Creator by trusting in Christ as your Savior? If so, here's a simple prayer you can use to express your faith:

Dear God,

I know that my sin has put a barrier
between You and me. Thank You for
sending Your Son, Jesus, to die in my place.
I trust in Jesus alone to forgive my sins, and
I accept His gift of eternal life. I ask Jesus to
be my personal Savior and the Lord of my
life. Thank You. In Jesus's name, amen.

If you've prayed this prayer or one like it and you wish to find out more about knowing God and His plan for you in the Bible, contact us at Insight for Living. Our contact information is on the following pages.

We Are Here for You

If you desire to find out more about knowing God and His plan for you in the Bible, contact us. Insight for Living provides staff pastors who are available for free written correspondence or phone consultation. These seminary-trained and seasoned counselors have years of experience and are well-qualified guides for your spiritual journey.

Please feel welcome to contact your regional Pastoral Ministries by using the information below:

United States

Insight for Living
Pastoral Ministries
Post Office Box 269000
Plano, Texas 75026-9000
USA
972-473-5097, Monday through Friday,
8:00 a.m. – 5:00 p.m. central time
www.insight.org/contactapastor

Canada

Insight for Living Canada
Pastoral Ministries
Post Office Box 2510
Vancouver, BC V6B 3W7
CANADA
1-800-663-7639
info@insightforliving.ca

Australia, New Zealand, and South Pacific

Insight for Living Australia
Pastoral Care
Post Office Box 443
Boronia, VIC 3155
AUSTRALIA
1300 467 444

United Kingdom and Europe

Insight for Living United Kingdom
Pastoral Care
PO Box 553
Dorking
RH4 9EU
UNITED KINGDOM
0800 915 9364
+44 (0)1306 640156
pastoralcare@insightforliving.org.uk

$\mathcal{E}$ndnotes

Opening Quote

1. Alister E. McGrath, *The Journey: A Pilgrim in the Lands of the Spirit*, 1st ed. (New York: Doubleday, 2000), 21–22.

Chapter 1

Taken from Charles R. Swindoll, "Strengthening Your Grip on Money," in *Strengthening Your Grip: Essentials in an Aimless World* (Dallas: Word, 1982), 71–87.

1. Joe Lewis, "Quotes," in Joe Lewis: The Official Web Site, http://www.cmgww.com/sports/louis/quotes.htm (accessed October 11, 2010).

2. Epicurus, as quoted in Grant Showerman, "Horace the Philosopher of Life," *The Classical Journal* 6, no. 7 (April 1911): 281.

3. William Shakespeare, *The Third Part of King Henry the Sixth*, 3.1.61–65, in *William Shakespeare: The Complete Works* (New York: Dorset Press, 1988), 79.

4. Ronald J. Sider, *Rich Christians in an Age of Hunger: Moving from Affluence to Generosity*, 5th ed. (Nashville: Thomas Nelson, 2005), 20.

5. William Barclay, *The Letters to Timothy*, The Daily Study Bible (Edinburgh: Saint Andrews Press, 1955), 152.

6. Alan Loy McGinnis, *The Friendship Factor* (Minneapolis: Augsburg, 1979), 30.

Chapter 2

Adapted from the message "Fanning the Financial Fire" in the series *A Minister Everyone Would Respect* by Charles R. Swindoll, as well as the chapter "Fanning the Financial Fire" in *A Minister Everyone Would Respect: A Study of 2 Corinthians 8–13*, (Plano, Tex.: Insight for Living, 2001), 8–16.

1. Oscar Wilde, *The Picture of Dorian Gray* (New York: Barnes & Noble Classics, 2003), 35.

2. Sophie Tucker, as quoted in Charles R. Swindoll, *The Tale of the Tardy Oxcart and 1,501 Other Stories* (Nashville: Word, 1998), 442.

3. Os Guinness, *The Call: Finding and Fulfilling the Central Purpose of Your Life* (Nashville: Word, 1998), 136.

4. John Wesley, "The Use of Money," in *Sermons on Several Occasions* (New York: G. Lane & C. B. Tippett, 1845), 446, http://books.google.com/books?id=2PI8AAAAcAAJ&printsec=frontcover&dq=sermons+on+several+occasions&hl=en&ei=0QS-TOWYE8L_lgeEs83iBw&sa=X&oi=book_result&ct=result&resnum=1&ved=0CDMQ6AEwAA#v=onepage&q&f=false (accessed October 19, 2010).

5. *Merriam-Webster's Collegiate Dictionary*, 11th ed. (Springfield, Mass.: Merriam-Webster, 2007), see "procrastinate."

6. Martha Snell Nicholson, "Treasures," in *Ivory Palaces* (Moody Publishers, 1946), 67.

Chapter 3

Taken from Charles R. Swindoll, "Sacrifice: Personal and Financial," in *The Owner's Manual for Christians: The Essential Guide for a God Honoring Life* (Nashville: Thomas Nelson, 2009), 195–211.

1. Jim Elliot, "October 28, 1949," in *The Journals of Jim Elliot*, ed. Elisabeth Elliot (Grand Rapids: Revell, 2004), 174.

2. Dallas Willard, *The Spirit of the Disciplines: Understanding How God Changes Lives* (San Francisco: Harper & Row, 1988), 175. Reprinted with permission of HarperCollins, Inc.

3. A. W. Tozer, *The Pursuit of God* (Camp Hill, Pa.: WingSpread, 2007), 28.

4. Elisabeth Elliot, *Through Gates of Splendor* (Carol Stream, Ill.: Tyndale House, 1981), 259.

Chapter 4

Adapted from the chapter "Love, Loans . . . and the Money Crunch" in *Hand Me Another Brick: How Effective Leaders Motivate Themselves and Others Bible Companion* (Nashville: W Publishing, 2006), 69–79.

1. Samuel Johnson, as quoted in James Boswell, *The Life of Samuel Johnson* (New York: Everyman's Library, 1906), 1044.

2. William Shakespeare, *Hamlet, Prince of Denmark*, 1.3.75, in *The Complete Works* (New York: Dorset Press, 1988), 675.

3. Francis Brown, S. R. Driver, and Charles A. Briggs, *The Brown-Driver-Briggs Hebrew and English Lexicon* (Peabody, Mass.: Hendrickson, 2006), 354.

4. Merrill F. Unger, *Unger's Bible Dictionary*, 3rd ed. (Chicago: Moody, 1974), 352.

5. Author Unknown, as quoted in *Gnomologia*, comp. Thomas Fuller (Delray Beach, Fla.: Levenger Press, 2008), 6.

6. For examples, see Ron Blue, *Master Your Money*, rev. and updated ed. (Nashville: Thomas Nelson, 1991), 19.

Resources for Probing Further

If you could gather every book ever written about money and lay them end-to-end, they would stretch for miles and miles, disappearing out of view over the horizon. Libraries are filled with volumes on how to make money, how to save money, how to invest money, how to shelter money from taxes, and how to give money away. The book you hold in your hands is different. This is a book about how to *think* about money—how to think about it from God's perspective as found in the Bible. But the Bible has more to say about money than this book could cover in four chapters, so we encourage you to dive deeply into Scripture and to further your study by looking into some of the resources listed below. Please keep in mind, we cannot always endorse everything a writer or ministry says in these works, so we encourage you to approach these and all other nonbiblical resources with wisdom and discernment.

Alcorn, Randy. *Managing God's Money: A Biblical Guide.* Grand Rapids: Tyndale House, 2011.

Blue, Ron, with Jeremy White. *The New Master Your Money: A Step-by-Step Plan for Gaining and Enjoying Financial Freedom.* 4th ed. Chicago: Moody Publishers, 2004.

Blue, Ron, with Jeremy White. *Surviving Financial Meltdown: Confident Decisions in an Uncertain World.* Grand Rapids: Tyndale House, 2009.

Ramsey, Dave. *The Money Answer Book.* Nashville: Thomas Nelson, 2010.

Ramsey, Dave. *The Total Money Makeover: A Proven Plan for Financial Fitness.* 3d. ed. Nashville: Thomas Nelson, 2009.

Swindoll, Charles R. *Strengthening Your Grip: Essentials in an Aimless World.* Dallas: Word Publishing, 1982.

Ordering *Information*

If you would like to order additional copies of *You and Your Money* or to order other Insight for Living resources, please contact the office that serves you.

United States

Insight for Living
Post Office Box 269000
Plano, Texas 75026-9000
USA
1-800-772-8888 (Monday through Friday, 7:00 a.m.–7:00 p.m. central time)
www.insight.org
www.insightworld.org

Canada

Insight for Living Canada
Post Office Box 2510
Vancouver, BC V6B 3W7
CANADA
1-800-663-7639
www.insightforliving.ca

Australia, New Zealand, and South Pacific

Insight for Living Australia
Post Office Box 443
Boronia, VIC 3155
AUSTRALIA
1300 467 444
www.insight.asn.au

United Kingdom and Europe

Insight for Living United Kingdom
PO Box 553
Dorking
RH4 9EU
UNITED KINGDOM
0800 915 9364
www.insightforliving.org.uk

Other International Locations

International constituents may contact the U.S. office
through our Web site (www.insightworld.org), mail
queries, or by calling +1-972-473-5136.